Work Smarter, Not Harder

Other books by Teruni Lamberg

Conducting Productive Meetings: How to Generate and Communicate Ideas for Innovation

Leaders Who Lead Successfully: Guidelines for Organizing to Achieve Innovation

Work Smarter, Not Harder

A Framework for Math Teaching and Learning

Teruni D. Lamberg

ROWMAN & LITTLEFIELD
London • New York

Published by Rowman & Littlefield
An imprint of The Rowman & Littlefield Publishing Group, Inc.
4501 Forbes Boulevard, Suite 200, Lanham, Maryland 20706
www.rowman.com

6 Tinworth Street, London SE11 5AL, United Kingdom

British Library Cataloguing in Publication Information Available

Library of Congress Control Number: 2019949860

∞™ The paper used in this publication meets the minimum requirements of American National Standard for Information Sciences—Permanence of Paper for Printed Library Materials, ANSI/NISO Z39.48–1992.

Printed in the United States of America

For my wonderful husband, Scott, our beloved son,
Zachary (Zack), and my parents

Contents

List of Tables

List of Video Clips

For full access to the videos listed here, visit https://textbooks.rowman.com/lamberg

Table 1.1 Video Information

	Video Clip	Length (Hr:Min:Sec)
Video 1.1	Second-Grade Review Lesson Two-Digit Addition with Regrouping	00:10:52
Video 1.2	Second-Grade Teacher Interview: Lesson Goals	00:01:21
Video 3.1	Subtraction and Regrouping Second-Grade Lesson Guided Lesson, Introducing a New Concept	00:17:50
Video 3.2	Teacher Interview: Second-Grade Scaffolding Student Thinking	00:02:37
Video 4.1	Fifth-Grade Teacher Interview	00:04:56
Video 5.1	Fifth-Grade Problem-Solving Lesson (Division/Decimals)	00:26:54
Video 5.2	Teacher Interview: Writing and Math in Fifth-Grade Lesson	00:04:07
Video 7.1	Two-Digit Addition with Regrouping Class 2	00:16:34
Video 7.2	Second-Grade Teacher Interview Class 2	00:05:07

Preface

Have you ever taught a lesson and discovered that students did not learn the material? The most important part of teaching is to help students learn math. However, this is not an easy task! The teacher must ensure that every student's needs are met and the standards are covered. Even if you spend 10 minutes with each student individually, it is physically impossible to do so within the hour!

Therefore, a whole class discussion becomes a powerful tool to help *all* students learn new information and clarify misconceptions and errors. A whole class discussion takes place when students and the teacher gather to discuss ideas and gain new insights. Students engage in discussion by sharing and critiquing each other's ideas to make new connections so that learning can take place.

First, we need to explore what is learning and how it takes place. According to the National Research Council (2000), learning takes place when students connect prior knowledge with new information. Therefore, teachers must create opportunities for students to make mathematical connections. A whole class discussion plays a vital role in accomplishing this goal. Learning happens in the classroom context that is influenced by the social interactions that take place within this setting.

When students develop *new* insights and learn something new in a meaningful way, they can *use* what they know in new or novel situations to solve problems. Knowledge becomes a tool. The National Research Council (2000) highlights that *transfer* is an essential part of learning. This takes place when students can explain what they are doing and make sense of things.

Research shows that students learn math through communication. When they discuss their ideas, listen to different perspectives, and engage in sense-making, they deepen their understanding of mathematics. Mathematics is more than following a series of steps and memorizing formulas. Mathematics is a "dynamic discipline focused on solving problems by thinking creatively, finding patterns, and reasoning logically" (Bray, 2011). Therefore, a problem-solving approach to learning supports students to engage in sense-making.

The Common Core Standards for Mathematical Practice (CCSSM, 2010) highlights a set of eight practices that support a problem-solving approach to teaching and sense-making. The discussion is an important part of learning math, and it is listed as the third math practice:

3. *Construct viable arguments and critique the reasoning of others.*

Mathematically proficient students understand and use stated assumptions, definitions, and previously established results in constructing arguments. They make conjectures and build a logical progression of statements to explore the truth of their conjectures. They can analyze situations by breaking them into cases and can recognize counter-examples. They justify their conclusions and communicate them to others and respond to the argument of others.

According to the Common Core Standards for Mathematical Practice, students must be able to explain and justify their thinking. Also, students should be able to explain *why* a mathematical statement is true or how a mathematical rule works.

COMMUNICATION AND MATHEMATICAL LEARNING

Learning math proficiently involves integrating different kinds of knowledge. The National Research Council (2001, P. 5) identified five strands for mathematical proficiency:

* *conceptual understanding*—comprehension of mathematical concepts, operations, and relations
* *procedural fluency*—skill in carrying out procedures flexibly, accurately, efficiently, and appropriately
* *strategic competence*—ability to formulate, represent, and solve mathematical problems
* *adaptive reasoning*—capacity for logical thought, reflection, explanation, and justification
* *productive disposition*—habitual inclination to see mathematics as sensible, useful, and worthwhile, coupled with a belief in diligence and one's efficacy.

Whole class discussions provide students with opportunities to explore these interrelated strands. When students share their reasoning and listen to different perspectives, they engage in *reflective* thought. Reflective thought involves carefully analyzing what is being said and making judgments and understanding how that new information fits with prior knowledge. On the other hand, if new information does not fit, a conscious effort is required to make sense of the new information (National Research Council, 2019). Typically, new learning and deeper understanding result. By sharing, explaining, and justifying ideas, students develop skills in reasoning and engage in sense-making.

WHOLE CLASS DISCUSSION AND STUDENT ACHIEVEMENT

Whole class discussions take time. Many teachers wonder if the time spent having discussions is justified when there is so much content to be covered in a short period. When students develop conceptual understanding of mathematical ideas, they *retain* what they learn and develop greater skills in math. If students forget how to solve a problem, they can figure it out. Whole class discussions can help students develop a conceptual understanding of math concepts and use more efficient strategies. Researchers highlight that focusing on different reasoning strategies leads to higher mathematical insights (Leinhardt & Steele, 2005; Stein, Engle, Smith, & Hughes, 2008).

On the other hand, when students simply memorize procedures for solving problems without understanding how or why they work, they are more likely to have difficulty remembering how to do problems (National Research Council, 2001). For example, students who memorize that $9 + 9 = 18$, without understanding what it means, are less likely to use that knowledge to solve additional problems. Helping students develop number sense allows students to make mathematical connections and successfully solve problems using efficient strategies.

Some teachers wonder if *all* the students benefit from whole class discussions. Sometimes some kids are more vocal than others. Connor, Michaels, and Chapin (2017) found in their study that whole class discussion using accountable talk was beneficial to the learning of the whole class. They compared a classroom with direct instruction against a classroom using discussion. These students learned the same content. Students in the class that incorporated discussion performed better on the post–math test than the students receiving direct instruction.

Some teachers worry that some students are more vocal while others are more silent during the discussion. They wonder if the kids who talk less still benefit from discussion. Connor et al. (2017) found that all students who participated in the whole class discussion instead of the direct instruction class performed better on the post-test. Discussion benefited the learning of all students, including those who were less vocal than others.

When students summarize information and explain what they are learning in a meaningful way, they can retain what they learn (National Research Council, 2019). During discussions, students get an opportunity to share their thinking and get feedback from others. Furthermore, they also get to expand their own thinking by reflecting on other perspectives, which allows them to gain a deeper understanding. Metacognition is an integral part of learning (National Research Council, 2019).

WHY SITUATE DISCUSSION IN THE PROCESS OF TEACHING

Whole class discussions must be situated in the *process of teaching* to optimize student learning. The *process of teaching* includes setting up the physical space, planning lessons, developing classroom routines, and facilitating discussions to help students make mathematical connections. Teachers naturally do these steps. But how these actions are carried out makes the difference in student learning. You will learn specific techniques in this book to create conditions to optimize learning.

The Common Core Standards for Mathematical Practice (CCSSM, 2010) outline the best practices to support mathematical learning. The Common Core Standards for Mathematical Practice (CCSSM, 2010) are the following:

- Make sense of problems and persevere in solving them.
- Reason abstractly and quantitatively.
- Construct viable arguments and critique the reasoning of others.
- Model with mathematics.
- Use appropriate tools strategically.
- Attend to precision.
- Look for and make use of structure.
- Look for and express regularity in repeated reasoning.

The *Whole Class Discussion Framework* presented in this book naturally integrates these practices as a natural part of teaching. Many teachers struggle to implement the Common Core Standards for Mathematical Practice because they try to implement each practice in a fragmented manner. For example, if a teacher is using a direct instruction method to show students step by step how to solve problems and then tries to have a discussion, the students may end up discussing the correct steps to solve the problem as opposed to engaging in sense-making.

Knowing how to integrate the standards for mathematical practice as a natural part of teaching and using them in whole class discussions. This book provides you with a framework that is easy to implement. This framework has been tested and revised in many classrooms over several years. The best part is that it works!

Teachers who have used this framework found that they were able to change their practice within a year and see results. Most importantly, when this framework is used with content-focused professional development, teachers discover that it increases student achievement! Not only has this framework been used with in-service teachers, but it has also been used with pre-service teachers as well who have provided feedback. This book outlines the *thinking process* you need to implement in effective discussions that support learning. Specifically, you will learn:

- how to set and organize your physical space for discussions
- the kinds of classroom routines that support thinking and communication
- how to plan effective lessons to help students make mathematical connections
- how to facilitate effective discussions that build on student thinking
- strategies for reflecting and improving your teaching.

HOW TO USE THIS BOOK

This book is designed to help you facilitate effective whole class discussions that support in-depth mathematical thinking and learning by thoughtfully attending to the components in the process of teaching. The goal is to optimize conditions to support student learning. Although the ideas presented in this book are aimed at mathematical discussions, these ideas can be adapted to other content areas as well. This book is intended to be used and reused as a tool. You may be an experienced teacher who is interested in fine-tuning your discussion. Or perhaps you are a pre-service teacher who is just starting the journey of becoming a teacher. Maybe, you are a math coach, a professional development coordinator, or a professor who is interested in supporting others to conduct effective whole class discussion.

This book can be used as a resource individually or as part of a book study group. Furthermore, you can choose tools and adapt them to meet your needs. Chapter 1 provides you with an overview of the thinking process needed to facilitate an effective whole class discussion. Each subsequent chapter describes various aspects of this process by synthesizing the research and providing practical strategies that can be directly applied in the classroom. Chapter 7 addresses how to evaluate your areas of strengths and weaknesses to refine and fine-tune your whole class discussions while getting the support you need. Each chapter contains some of the following features:

- A **Synthesis of Research** with concrete examples of what it looks like in the classroom.
- A bulleted list of **Strategies for Your Classroom** that you can directly apply in the classroom based on the ideas discussed in the chapter.
- **Self-Reflection Questions** that are designed to help you reflect on your classroom.
- A **Book Study Guide** that provides you with guidelines on how to use the tools and resources to deepen your understanding of the key ideas presented in each chapter, make connections to real classrooms. This book study guide can be used individually or as a group.
- **Video clips referenced throughout the text** that include examples of whole class discussions, teacher interviews, and student interviews from a variety of grade levels and schools.
- **Strategies for the classroom and worksheets from this book, including rubrics, self-evaluation tools, and questions for discussion include:**
    - **Strategies for the Classroom.** Key ideas from each chapter are provided in a bulleted list as specific strategies that can be tried out in the classroom.
    - **Reflecting on Videos.** Questions are provided for the viewer to think about each video clip. These questions correspond to the content presented in each chapter. These questions can be used along with the Video Study Guides.
    - **Reflecting on Practice.** These tools are intended to help the teacher to identify areas of strengths and weaknesses in whole class discussions. Once areas for growth are identified, the book and other resources can be used as a support to improve teaching.
    - **Rubrics and Checklists.** These tools are designed to monitor and provide feedback on classroom discussions.

How to Adapt This Book for Pre-Service Teachers

Pre-service students will get an image of what a whole class discussion that supports learning looks like and gain insights into planning lessons with discussions in mind. Also, this book will be a great resource when they enter the classroom. I have found it helpful to model the components of the framework throughout the semester and make students explicitly reflect on these aspects. This book is also an excellent supplement to any field experience class where pre-service teachers are working with real students.

Acknowledgments

I would like to thank my editor Dr. Tom Koerner for his continued support of my work. He is a delight to work with. I am thankful to Shaun Sanchez, Ana Sanchez, Claudia Bertolone-Smith, Marlene Moyer, Kelsey Rivara, Megan Tilton, Channon Toles, and Bonnie Akbar, who were gracious enough to let me videotape them. They truly are dedicated teachers who care about teaching and helping other teachers as well. These are real classrooms. These videos illustrate what a discussion looks like. You can learn so many things by watching real classrooms such as things that worked well and the challenges they faced.

The manuscript developed out of many ideas. I appreciate the many conversations with and constructive feedback I received from teachers and others during the process of writing my manuscript. I would like to thank the Lemelson Cohort teachers and the Nevada Mathematics Project teachers and also Kathy Dees, Denise Trakas, Dave Brancamp, Tracy Gruber, Heather Crawford-Ferre, Peggy Lakey, Edward Keppelman, Diana Moss, Linda Gillette-Koyen, Mitchell Nathan and Rebecca Bondocco. I would also like to thank my parents who inspired me that anything was possible to achieve if you set your mind to it. I would also like to thank Carlie Wall and Naviya Gowtham for their support in the development of this manuscript. Finally, I could not have done this without the love and support of my husband and son! They mean the world to me.

Chapter 1

The Whole Class Discussion Framework

Whole class discussions must be situated in the *process of teaching* to optimize opportunities for students to learn math. Many years ago, a teacher shared with me that she can get discussions going into her classroom. I was so excited to hear that until she sighed and said, "I am still not getting results in student learning."

I asked her what curriculum she used. She explained, "I don't use any." She taught lessons by gathering a variety of lesson planning resources from different sources. I asked her what she did to sequence the lessons. She threw her hands up in the air in frustration and said, "I don't have time to do this!" She indicated that she had time only to think about each lesson in isolation. Sequencing within and across lessons was something she did not have time to think about.

This conversation had a profound influence on me. My work has involved working with teachers over the past 18 years across the country to improve teaching through professional development and conducting research. My mission is to support teachers not only to have great discussions, but also to have great conversations that result in student learning!

Therefore, I changed how I was working with this group of teachers. We started to look at research and examine the components in the *process of teaching* to help students learn math. The Whole Class Discussion Framework described in this book has been tested and refined by hundreds of teachers from the Northeastern Nevada Math Project, Nevada Math Project, and several Lemelson STEM cohorts at the University of Nevada, Reno. Many pre-service teachers provided feedback as well.

COMPONENTS OF THE PROCESS OF TEACHING

The following are the components of the process of teaching:
* designing the physical space
* developing classroom routines
* planning lessons
* facilitating discussions
* reflecting on the effectiveness and next steps.

This framework captures what teachers naturally do. How these components are enacted in the classroom is what makes the difference! What we discovered is that attending to the *process of teaching* changes classroom practice. All these components listed must work together to optimize opportunities for student learning. Whole class discussion is an integral part of this process.

Implementing the ideas presented in the book takes time, but it is well worth the effort. Teachers that I have worked with reported that not only did teaching become easier, but it also helped improve students' test scores! You can *work smarter* by making more *targeted decisions* to support the individual needs of your students.

This chapter provides an overview of the components of the Whole Class Discussion Framework, and each subsequent chapter includes detailed information about various parts of the framework and strategies for you to implement them in the classroom. First, we will examine a whole class discussion from Mr. Sanchez's second-grade class.

There are three levels of sense-making that help students make mathematical connections during a discussion. These three levels are so easy to remember and use. Moreover, you will be naturally integrating the Standards for Mathematical Practice in the Common Core Mathematics Standards (CCSSM, 2010) in your teaching.

THREE LEVELS OF SENSE-MAKING FRAMEWORK
FOR DISCUSSION

* First Level of Sense-Making: *Make thinking explicit*
* Second Level of Sense-Making: *Analyze each other's solutions*
* Third Level of Sense-Making: *Make "big idea" explicit*

Watch classroom video 1.1: Second-Grade Review Lesson (Two-Digit Addition with Regrouping) https://textbooks.rowman.com/lamberg

A group of second graders are gathered together in front of an interactive board. Students excitedly look at the colorful display containing a digital place value mat and a 100 chart. Mr. Sanchez points and says, "We are on 60, and how many until 100?" He points out that they have been in school for 60 days. A student points to 60 and moves her hand to the corresponding number and starts counting "60, 70, 80, 90, and 100." Mr. Sanchez clarifies, "*How many* until 100?" By asking this question, he refocuses the students to think about the meaning of addition as opposed to a number sequence. The students explore solving the problem using the virtual place value mat. He clears the interactive board and writes 38 + 52 (see Figure 1.1) and asks students to mentally add the numbers together.

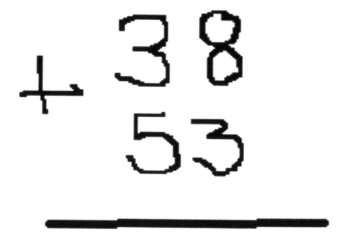

Figure 1.1. Two digit Addition Problem

The students must first solve a problem before a whole class discussion. This process involves students developing a shared understanding of a problem. This problem was carefully chosen because it is a two-digit addition problem with regrouping. Students had previously practiced this concept. Therefore, by solving this problem, students had the opportunity to use their *prior knowledge* and revisit the meaning of regrouping. When interviewed, Mr. Sanchez shared that he usually likes to start his lesson with mental math. The goal for this part of the lesson and discussion was to help students figure out "which strategy will be most efficient." He knew that students had the background knowledge to be able to solve this problem mentally.

First Level of Sense-Making: Make Thinking Explicit

Students solved the problem mentally and enthusiastically raised their hands to indicate that they were ready to share their thinking. Mr. Sanchez had given the class some time to think through the problem quietly. He asks the class for answers to the problem of adding 38 + 52. One student raises his hand and says, "80." Mr. Sanchez asks the class if they have other answers. Another student responds, "91."

Mr. Sanchez records both answers on the interactive board as class answers. Even though there are 19 students, there are only two different types of class answers. At this point, Mr. Sanchez must decide on how to proceed with the discussion. He chooses to have the first student explain his reasoning on how he got 80.

The following is a summary of each student's explanation. When analyzing each other's answers, students had to think about the following solutions:

1. adding tens digits together to make 80, but forgot to add the ones unit
2. adding the digits 3 and 5 in the tens column to make 80, then adding 8 and counting up 3 to make 90.
3. adding the tens digits to make 80 and then adding the ones digits together to make 11 and adding the numbers together.

During the *Make thinking explicit* phase students share their answers. The goal is to understand and evaluate each other's thinking. Typically, there are about three to five different ways the class is thinking about the problem. Over 100 teachers brought student work to professional development sessions in the Nevada Mathematics Project. Each teacher took a problem and sorted them into piles based on student reasoning. These teachers discovered that there were typically about two to five different types of thinking.

Knowing that there are only about two to five different ways of thinking makes teaching a lot less stressful than having to deal with 20 different answers. Therefore, the teacher must decide what answers should be shared in the discussion and how to meaningfully sequence the explanations. The purpose is to help students make meaningful connections.

The goal is not to have every student share his or her answer. Rather, the purpose is to make visible the kinds of thinking students can engage in a discussion and make mathematical connections. Typically having students share about three different answers makes efficient use of class time for discussion and analysis. Furthermore, it keeps the whole class engaged.

Second Level of Sense-Making: Analyze Each Other's Solutions

Whole class discussions must engage students in critical thinking (Chapin, O'Conner, & Anderson, 2009; Smith & Stein, 2011). Analyzing how other students are thinking about the problem requires students to think about the underlying mathematics. For example, in Mr. Sanchez's class, after the first student explains how he got 80 as his solution, another student points out that he disagrees with his answer. He explains that the student did not solve the whole problem by using *all* the numbers in the problem.

Another student points out that he did not start at 38 and add 53. Both students visualized the problem differently. The student who had answered "80" had added the tens together. The class did not see what he was thinking. Mr. Sanchez asks, "Did he do any part of the problem correctly?" The class initially responds "No!" However, when Mr. Sanchez points and asks, "What is 30 and 50?" The students realize that the student had added the 10s together and forgotten to add the ones. This is an example, which illustrates how misconceptions and errors can be addressed through discussion. The whole class discussion gives students opportunities to discuss *why* something does or does not make sense.

Many students raise their hands to share how they got 91. Mr. Sanchez gets two students to share their thinking. He tells one student that he overheard how he was thinking about the question. Therefore, he wanted him to share his thinking with the class by writing his answer on the interactive board and explaining the reasoning. When Mr. Sanchez had asked students to individually solve the problems and share, he was carefully observing and thinking about how to use the information to support student learning through discussion.

The student writes on the interactive board and explains that he got 80, added 8 to it and got 88. Then he counted on his fingers and added three more. He writes out 88, 89, and 91. The teacher revoices the strategy, and the class agrees that the answer makes sense. Another student explains that she added 30 with 50 and got 80. Then she added 8 and 3 together and got 11. She wrote 80 + 11 and indicated 91. However, she did not align the 91 directly under the appropriate place value column.

Mr. Sanchez said, "I kind of disagree with her answer. Can anybody see why I might disagree with her answer?" Students raised their hands. The student looks back and reflects on what she wrote. Another student explains that the problem is "she put her ones in the tens place." The teacher scaffolds the student's explanation by pointing and explaining that this is 900, and tens go under tens and ones go under ones. The student nods in agreement and realizes her mistake. The teacher asks her to fix her mistake, and she does it successfully.

Students need to listen with an open mind and be willing to change their answer if it does not make sense. For example, the student who had written 91 in the incorrect place value location realized her mistake and was able to fix her thinking. The whole class discussion opens students to different possibilities that they may not have thought about individually or with small groups. The social interaction leads students to think, reflect, and refine their thought processes (Chapin, Conner, & Anderson, 2009).

Third Level of Sense-Making: Develop New Mathematical Insights

A discussion must lead to the development of "big mathematical ideas" and skills that students can understand and use to solve other problems. This third level of sense-making is a critical part of supporting student learning. It is not essential that students memorize the answer to the addition problem. Students need to understand place value and addition strategies that could be used to solve additional problems.

During this phase, the teacher can scaffold student thinking in a meaningful way by building on a student's prior knowledge and sense-making. The teacher made explicit the meaning of digits, place value, and addition strategies by building on students' prior knowledge and problem-solving strategies. Mr. Sanchez summarized the lesson as follows to reach a shared understanding:

> *MR. SANCHEZ:* We need to watch everything right? The columns are there for a reason! What did you catch yourself on the right at the beginning?
>
> *STUDENTS:* The tens and ones.
>
> *MR. SANCHEZ:* You went to call the tens ones, she said I added the 3 and then she caught herself. If it is a 3 (pointing to the 30), it is a what?
>
> *STUDENTS:* Value?
>
> *MR. SANCHEZ:* It is not its value.
>
> *STUDENTS:* It is a digit!
>
> *MR. SANCHEZ:* If it is a digit you call it 3. It can be 3.
>
> *STUDENTS:* Tens.
>
> *MR. SANCHEZ:* So, can be 30. But it cannot be 300 because this digit where it is now can be called, three tens or 30.
>
> *STUDENTS:* Thirty.
>
> *MR. SANCHEZ:* That is it, that's its name.

The "big idea" that is made explicit is that digits can have different values and be represented with place value notation. He specifically made explicit the difference between the ones digit and the tens digit. Strategies for addition were also made explicit.

If students think that the teacher is the only one with the correct answer, they are not likely to be mentally engaged or open to thinking about mathematics. Students must think about how to individually approach the problem. Besides, they must also understand how other students approach them. This helps them make sense of their thinking and mathematics. Students in Mr. Sanchez's class were actively listening and participating. They were able to share their reasoning as well as critique the reasoning of their peers.

Whole class discussions must lead to the development of a more sophisticated understanding of mathematics and build on student thinking by addressing different strategies and errors that students make. Classroom discussion time must be used *effectively* and *efficiently* to support student learning. The Table 1.1 listed here distinguishes the characteristics of a discussion that promotes and does not support conceptual understanding.

Table 1.1   Characteristics of Effective and Ineffective Whole Class Discussions

Effective Discussion	Ineffective Discussion
The discussion is open-ended with many opportunities for students to present multiple perspectives. Students can explain *how* and *why* problem-solving strategies work.	The discussion is closed, with only one right approach to solving the problem. Students explain the steps to solve the problem but are unable to explain *why* or *how* it works.
Students engage in sense-making and explore a problem or issue.	Students passively listen to the teacher.
The purpose of the discussion is to explore and understand a mathematical problem or issue.	Teacher shows students the steps on how to solve problems. Students copy and use the steps to solve problems without understanding why.
The teacher acts as a facilitator by scaffolding and guiding the discussion to support students to make mathematical connections. Students explore *how* to solve problems as well as *why* the approach works.	The teacher explains the steps to problem-solving as students listen passively or give the correct answers without further explanation.

Planning a Whole Class Discussion

Orchestrating an effective whole class discussion involves creating the physical and social environment to support discussions, preparing the lesson, identifying a topic and a problem to discuss, allowing students to share reasoning, and using guided questions to help facilitate mathematical connections. The ultimate goal of teaching is to support student learning.

Three Levels of Lesson Planning

1. Long-Term Goals

• Examine standards: Identify concepts and skills students need to learn.
• Examine curriculum: Look at sequencing and how it connects to standards.

2. Short-Term Goals

• Look at the curriculum unit: Identify what students need to learn and what needs to be assessed.
• Plan for the week: Make a five-day unit plan (lay out a learning trajectory) and consider formative/summative assessment data and math content covered for the week.
• Plan the lesson (daily): Identify lesson goals and plan how to structure class time to meet lesson goal. The purpose should drive structure. Adapt lesson based on assessment (formative and summative data).

3. Planning/Adapting while Teaching

• Adapt lesson based on student reasoning and sense-making while teaching.
• Facilitate the discussion using three levels of sense-making to support mathematical connections and learning.
• Formatively assess to make decisions.

A whole class discussion focuses on one concept or goal; however, it is also part of a larger conversation that takes place over time. When students see connections within a lesson and across lessons, they develop deeper mathematical connections. Therefore, planning begins with setting a clear goal and purpose that fit in with a larger purpose. (Chapters 4, 5 and 6 discuss lesson planning and sequencing in more detail.) During this process, the teacher identifies the concepts and skills that students should develop and selects tasks for students to engage in. Also, the teacher anticipates student reasoning, errors, and misconceptions that can emerge during the lesson.

   Watch video 1.2: Second Grade Teacher Interview: Lesson goals.
https://textbooks.rowman.com/lamberg

   Mr. Sanchez's interview provides insights into his thinking and decision-making process as a teacher. He explained that he likes to structure his lesson by starting with mental math as illustrated in video 1.1. He shared that he was currently working on addition with regrouping with his students. Mr. Sanchez clearly articulated the mathematical content goals for the lesson.

In addition, he also identified the kinds of problem-solving skills that he wants his students to develop. The first part of the lesson was set up to help students understand place value and regrouping so that he could scaffold their thinking to solve subtraction with regrouping within a 100 problem. Mr. Sanchez connected these mathematical goals to the lesson to the second-grade-level standards. He was able to articulate what mathematical concepts he wanted students to understand. Also, problems and activities were carefully selected to align with students' background knowledge. By thinking about the problems to pose, the materials to use, and the sequence of the lesson to optimize mathematical connections, Mr. Sanchez laid out a learning trajectory for his students. His decisions were based on the standards, the curriculum, and assessment of his students' learning needs.

CHAPTER SUMMARY

Discussions must be situated in the process of teaching to get results in student learning. The purpose of a whole class discussion is support students' developmental, conceptual, and procedural understanding of mathematics through problem-solving, reasoning, communication, and sense-making. An effective whole class discussion includes three phases: (1) making thinking explicit, (2) analyzing each other's solutions, and (3) developing new mathematical insights. Whole class discussions contribute to efficient use of class time to support student learning.

The next section provides a synthesized summary of the whole class discussion framework that considers the *process of teaching*. The framework is aligned with the Common Core Standards for Mathematical Practice (CCSSM, 2010). The framework is only two-and-a-half-page long! The goal is for you to work smarter, not harder! Use this framework as a tool to reflect and fine-tune your teaching. Figure out what is working and what is not and use the strategies outlined in this book as a toolbox to fine-tune your teaching!

                                     Chapter 1

WHOLE CLASS DISCUSSION FRAMEWORK

The ultimate goal of teaching is to support student *learning*!

1. What should my students learn?
2. What are they learning?
3. Am I effective?

Table 1.2   The Whole Class Discussion Framework: Checklist of Progress

	Not Met	Work in Progress	Working Great	To do list	Tools from Whole Class Discussion book
Setting up the Classroom					(Chapter 2) * Checklist
Setting up Physical Space					
Cultivating Classroom Environment/Routines				**Note:** Routines for (Communicating/Listening Takes place during whole class discussion. These routines take time to develop.)	(Chapter 3) **Strategies for Your Classroom, Ideas for Developing classroom Routines**
Routines for Preparing for Discussion					Standards of Mathematical Practice 1,4,5,7,8
Routines for Communicating					Standards of Mathematical Practice 2,3
Routines for Listening/Reflecting					Standards of Mathematical Practice 1
Lesson Planning				**Note:** the Third level of planning takes place during lesson/discussion. The purpose of the first two levels of planning is to situate the discussion in larger goals to support deeper learning.	(Chapter 4 & 5) **Strategies for Your Classroom (Three Levels of Planning)**
First level Planning: Long-term Goals Examine Standards Examine Curriculum Scope and Sequence					Concept Map Rubric for Unit Planning

Second Level of Planning: Short Term Goals Plan Curriculum Unit Plan for Week (Unit Plan) Use assessment to lay out activities Anticipate student Reasoning					* Rubric for 5E Lesson Plan: Level 2
Third Level of Planning (Adapting discussion to support student understanding/needs) Plan Lesson based on purpose and goals Adapt the lesson while teaching based on student reasoning					*Rubric for Planning the Discussion: Level 3
The Discussion Supporting Mathematical Connections				**Note:** These levels of Sense-Making make up the Whole discussion. The teacher poses a problem and issue for the class to discuss. The teacher uses questions to help students make mathematical connections. Students communicate their ideas; reflect on their ideas and others being presented to make connections. (See classroom routines section).	(Chapter 6) (Identify a topic for discussion based on goals)
Three Levels of Sense-Making					**Strategies for Your Classroom: The Three Levels of Sense-Making**
Phase 1: Making Thinking explicit					Standards of Mathematical Practice 2, 3, 4
Phase II: Analyzing Each other's solutions					Helping students make connections from low-level strategies to sophisticated strategies S Address Errors/Misconceptions Standards of Mathematical Practice 1,3,4,6,7,8

12   *Chapter 1*

Phase III: Developing New Mathematical Insights					and create a record Standards of Mathematical Practice 1,2,4,5,6,7,8
				Improving Teaching Through Reflection	
Reflecting on Your Teaching (Making Teaching Visible)	What are you currently doing?	What is working/what is not?			(Chapter 7)
Making Teaching Visible Reflect on Strengths and Weaknesses					See: Reflecting on Practice Questions throughout chapters & *Reflecting on Your Practice Worksheets in End of Chapter Study Guides

Next Steps:

STUDY GUIDE

What is a whole class discussion, and how does it support learning?

REFLECTING ON CLASSROOM VIDEO CASES

Watch video 1.2: Second-Grade Teacher interview: Lesson Goals.

Mr. Sanchez is about to teach a lesson for second graders. He discusses his goals for the lesson.

Questions

1. What are Mr. Sanchez's goals for the lesson? How do these goals connect with the standards?
2. How does he plan and sequence activities in his lessons?
3. How does he account for student thinking as he plans the lesson?
4. What are teachers' perspectives on the role of whole class discussions as a means of supporting mathematical learning?

Watch classroom video Two-Digit Addition with Regrouping https://textbooks.rowman.com/lamberg

PHYSICAL SPACE

1. How was the space designed? How did the design contribute to the discussion?

CLASSROOM ROUTINES

1. What classroom routines did you observe?
2. What management strategies did Mr. Sanchez use?

LESSON PLANNING

1. What mathematical goals did you observe that connect to standards?
2. What lesson activities took place in what sequence?
3. How did the lesson activities contribute to learning?

THE DISCUSSION

1. How did Mr. Sanchez scaffold student thinking?
2. What errors and misconceptions arose in the lesson? How were these resolved?
3. Identify the three levels of sense-making in the discussion. How did that contribute to student learning and the making of connections?

   - Make thinking explicit
   - Analyze each other's solutions
   - Develop new mathematical insights.

4. Did the students gain new mathematical insights because of this discussion? Why or why not?
5. Did students make connections between each other's explanations? If so, how did this happen?
6. What caused the student to self-correct his answer?
7. What was the role of the teacher?
8. How did the students participate in this discussion?
9. Did learning take place?

Think about how whole class discussions can support mathematical learning. Reflect on your teaching as you read through each chapter and identify what levels of the framework you are currently implementing.

Chapter 1

STRATEGIES FOR YOUR CLASSROOM

**How and When to Use Whole Class Discussion
to Support Learning**

Use whole class discussion to:

- introduce new mathematical ideas
- address misconceptions and errors
- make deeper mathematical connections
- develop more efficient strategies.

Whole class discussion should

- focus on sense-making, reasoning, and communication
- build on small-group and partner talk
- address the needs of diverse learners
- help students develop new mathematical insights

Chapter 2

Design the Physical Space for Discussions

Best discussions take place where there is a spirit of inquiry and an environment of trust.

(Spiegel, 2005, emphasis added)

Figure 2.0.   Organizing Space for Discussion

DESIGN ELEMENTS FOR CLASSROOM SPACE

A well-designed classroom space enhances discussions. Design elements for organizing the physical space for productive discussions include creating a focal point, a place for students and the teacher to gather, ease of access to tools and materials, and a space to display student work (see Figures 2.0 and 2.1).

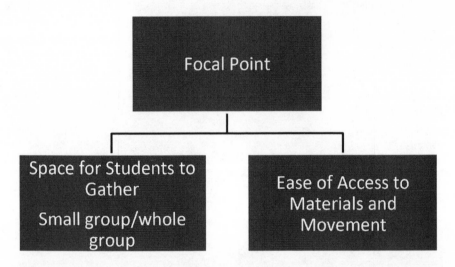

The physical space influences the kinds of interactions that can take place during a discussion. Figure 2.2 is an example of how one teacher organized her physical space for whole class discussion.

Students are physically gathered together on the carpet space designated for a whole class discussion. Students have their math journals in their hands so that they can refer to them when explaining their thinking. All can see the easel, on which the teacher has written "2/3 = 6/9, true or false?" The teacher is seated behind the students facing the chart paper. A student shares her thinking of why she believes this equation is true by pointing to the chart paper that shows "2/3 = 6/9." Other students listen intently to her explanation.

The chart paper from the previous day's discussion hangs on the bulletin board next to the easel. The physical space influences the kinds of interactions that can take place during a discussion. The chart paper easel creates a focal point for students to look at during the conversation. The carpet space becomes an intimate setting for students to gather together. The chart paper on the board displaying student work makes it possible to refer to previous discussions and solutions.

Not every classroom will have adequate room for a carpet space for students to gather. This is especially true when the students are older. Therefore, consider positioning the desks so that students can view the focal point. This design will help keep the student's attention. If an interactive board is unavailable, the focal point can be the whiteboard or a chart paper easel.

Self-Reflection Question

1. How does the space in your classroom contribute to the small-group and whole class discussions?

Specifically reflect on the following:

- Is there a focal point? Can everyone see the board/interactive board/ chart paper?
- Do students have access to materials?
- Can students physically transition from one activity such as sitting in small groups to large groups easily? Are there clear pathways for students to physically move around the room?
- Do students know where to sit?
- Is there space to display multiple representations for analysis?

DESIGNING A FUNCTIONAL SPACE FOR DISCUSSIONS

At the beginning of the school year, teachers prepare their classrooms by making decisions about the arrangement of student desks, teacher desk, materials, and use of space for activities and meetings. The size of the room influences decisions, the number of students, and the furniture available. In addition to creating a warm and inviting environment, teachers need to consider the *functionality* of the space. Functionality involves thinking about how to use the space. Consider how to design spaces for small groups and whole groups to meet.

Designing Space for Small Groups

When small groups gather, they need a shared working space that allows face-to-face interaction (see figure 2.3). Individual desks can be grouped so that students face each other, or larger desks that can seat several students can be used. The teacher should be able to walk around the groups to formatively assess and monitor the discussions by observing students.

Figure 2.3.   Students gather in Small Groups

Designing Space for Whole Class Discussions

Design elements that facilitate whole class discussions include a focal point, seating arrangements without distractions, and access to tools and materials. If you have space available, create a separate area for the whole class to gather together for discussion. Students (particularly younger students) are more focused on the discussion if they are physically gathered close together. This minimizes distractions and makes it easier to make eye contact and evaluate how students are participating in the discussion.

CREATING A FOCAL POINT

A *focal point* is what students look at such as a chart paper easel, whiteboard, or interactive board when they are engaging in a discussion. It should be in a place where students can demonstrate their thinking and simultaneously view multiple representations to make comparisons. If a student is writing a solution to a problem that some students are unable to see, then the visual representation becomes a useless tool for discussion. It is much easier to understand someone else's thinking, critique thinking, and compare solutions if you can visually see what they are thinking. Furthermore, students or the teacher can point to the parts of the visual representation they are talking about to focus the groups' attention.

Researchers Nathan and Knuth (2003) found that when the teacher physically removed herself from the center of the focal point and sat behind the group, the students began to talk to each other more instead of speaking directly to the teacher to answer her questions. Students took ownership of the conversation when the teacher was not the center of the discussion. Sometimes, it is necessary for the teacher to stand in front of the group to discuss or scaffold ideas especially during a guided lesson. Therefore, teachers need to consider where they should sit or stand during the discussion and how they can quickly move to the focal point if necessary.

Self-Reflection Questions

1. Where do you usually stand during a classroom lesson?
2. When should you remove yourself from the center to allow students to engage in conversation with each other?

ACCESS TO MATERIALS

Students can also use physical tools to represent their ideas and communicate their thinking (NCTM, 2000). They need manipulatives, pens, and paper, as well as access to chart paper and a dry erase board. Making these materials accessible close to the focal point or having a place where students can easily access these tools will minimize transition times.

The shelves in figure 2.4 contain many kinds of materials that are easily accessible to the teacher and other students. Students can see what types of tools are available and know where to return them after discussion. A poster or bulletin board visible to the whole group can display key vocabulary words or guidelines for communication.

Figure 2.4.   Shelves Containing Materials

Access to Technology

Technology, such as LCD projectors, interactive whiteboards, document cameras, class websites, and computer software, enhances teaching and learning of mathematics. Technology can be effectively integrated as part of discussions if it is located by the focal point. Technology may eliminate the need to create and store chart paper records. Student work can be displayed in a document camera and saved for later use. Students can write on the interactive board and augment the written work. If you have an interactive board with a document camera, make sure the camera is easily accessible close to the focal point.

Displaying and Saving Students' Work

One of the challenges teachers often face in teaching is time. During the whole class discussion, you need to decide if there is enough time to finish the conversation. If the bell rings before the conversation ends, student work should be saved so that it can be easily accessed the next day. One teacher uses clothes rack with coat hangers to save work as illustrated in Figure 2.5. Previously created ideas can be accessed to continue the conversation.

I have observed many lessons where students immediately erase their drawings soon after they explain their thinking to the class. Unfortunately, this

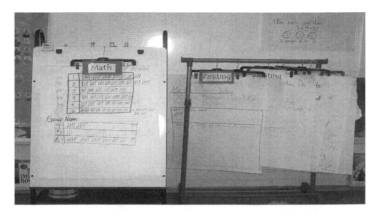

Figure 2.5. Saving Work for Later Use

prevents students from being able to compare each other's answers or revisit the ideas later. Therefore, think about how to save student work as needed. Documents can be saved electronically. Periodically look at your classroom. Is this design working? Does space need to be rearranged or decluttered?

Mr. Sanchez had a well-designated carpet space for discussion. The focal point was the interactive board. A carpet was placed in front of the interactive board during the first part of the lesson. The students sat on the rug facing the board. This way, they could see what was being shared on the interactive board and could participate in the discussion. Figure 2.6 illustrates how the students sat for the first part of the lesson.

Mr. Sanchez's second part of the lesson involved working with manipulatives. He wanted this to be a guided lesson to scaffold students' thinking of

Figure 2.6. Mr. Sanchez Class Gather for Discussion

place value when working with subtraction. Therefore, Mr. Sanchez had his students sit around the edges of the rectangular carpet. Colored dots indicated where students should sit (see figure 2.7.). The dots helped students know where they should sit for an interactive carpet lesson and prevented students from bumping into each other or pushing and shoving to find a spot.

The materials needed for the lesson were organized in individual Tupperware containers. Students knew exactly where to get materials. Mr. Sanchez had given very specific and explicit instructions for transitions. This made the

Figure 2.7.   Students Sit on Colored Dots

transitions very smooth from a classroom management perspective. Smooth transitions prevent wasting precious instructional time.

CHAPTER SUMMARY

A whole class discussion is much easier to facilitate when the physical space of the classroom is designed with discussions in mind. Specifically, there needs to be space for students to gather around the focal point during the discussion to display and analyze multiple representations.

Materials and tools for discussion must be readily available so that the flow of conversation is not interrupted. Also, the teacher must think about how to save student work for future reference. The classroom must also be designed for space for individuals and partners, small groups, and whole class discussions. A well-designed physical space for discussion saves time in transitioning from individual work to small groups to whole class discussions. Math lessons are much more productive if a teacher has excellent classroom management techniques.

STUDY GUIDE

Think about how the design of the physical space of your classroom can support discussions. Try some of the ideas listed in the "Strategies for Your Classroom" section. If you have your own classroom, you can make sure that your classroom layout addresses the bulleted points. If you do not have your classroom just yet, try to imagine how you would like to organize your space. Draw a diagram of how you would like to organize your space and get feedback from peers. Examine your classroom or the drawing against the checklist provided.

STRATEGIES FOR YOUR CLASSROOM

Considerations for Organizing the Physical Space

Small-Group Discussion Space

- common space to work where students can see each other
- space for the teacher to walk around and observe student conversations
- clear paths for students to transition to whole group space such as a carpet

Large-Group Discussion Space

- the focal point that can be viewed by all students (e.g., white board, interactive board, easel with chart paper)
- a place to display multiple student works
- space for students to sit a facing the focal point
- a path for students to walk back and forth to the focal point to share answers
- a place for the teacher to stand in front and back of the group as needed during the discussion
- storage place for materials and supplies close to the focal point
- access to technology (e.g., doc cam and interactive boards)
- a place or technology to store student work for future reference

REFLECTING ON PRACTICE

Designing Classroom Space

1. Draw a diagram of how you can organize your classroom space.

2. Describe the *functional* features of your space.

3. What technology and tools do you have available in your class for discussion? Are they located in a place with easy access during the discussion?

CHECKLIST OF PHYSICAL LAYOUTS FOR CLASSROOM DISCUSSIONS

Use this checklist (see Table 2.1) to evaluate your classroom or ask a colleague or math coach to provide you with their impressions.

Table 2.1   Checklist for Organizing the Physical Layout of the Classroom

	Observed	Notes—To-do list
Small Group		
Space for small groups to meet to discuss		
Space for the teacher to walk around the room and observe students		
Paths for students to walk to the whole group space		
Whole Group		
Focal point visible to the whole group with a place to write ideas and representations		
Place for students to sit		
A place for the teacher to stand/sit in front of and away from the focal point		
Access to technology for discussions		
Access to materials and supplies for discussion		
A place to share multiple student works		
A place to store student work for future reference (could include technology)		
Overall Effectiveness		
Areas that need improvement		
Areas that need decluttering		

Chapter 3

Classroom Routines for Discussions

Effective teachers have invisible procedures. Observers in the classroom don't see them, but they know they exist. That is why effective teachers' classrooms run so smoothly.

(Wong & Wong, 2009, p. 195, emphasis added)

The classroom social environment can either stimulate productive discussions or stifle thinking and sharing of ideas. How students interact with each other and with the teacher matters. Students who are encouraged to participate freely in thought-provoking whole class discussions will share their ideas and opinions, challenge each other's thinking, and help the whole class develop mathematical insights. Students share their thoughts when they feel safe and supported in the classroom environment. Therefore, the teacher needs to create a supportive *classroom community* that facilitates productive discussions.

BUILDING A SUPPORTIVE CLASSROOM COMMUNITY

Students feel connected to each other and trust each other in supportive classroom communities. They work together for the common good to support their learning as well as their peers (Hardin, 2011). Patrick, Turner, Meyer, and Midgley (2003) discovered that students who felt emotionally and intellectually supported performed better in mathematics and engaged in class discussions. In contrast, they discovered that students who did not feel supported used "avoidance tactics" when it was time to do the math. Therefore, Patrick et al. (2003) concluded that teachers who create supportive environments are more successful in involving students in math discussion than those who do not.

Teachers connected with students and built a supportive learning environment by using humor, revealing something personal about themselves, showing respect for students, sharing an enthusiasm for learning mathematics, and voicing expectations that all students can learn (Patrick, Turner, Meyer, & Midgley, 2003). Building a classroom learning community leads to a well-functioning classroom. The teacher must create classroom rituals, allow students to get to know each other, and promote kindness and caring (Larrivee, 2008).

Not only does the teacher's interaction with students matter, but how classmates treat each other also makes a difference. When students feel threatened, they do not share their ideas (Jenson, 2008). They don't like to feel criticized and judged on their abilities. Students need to see themselves as "helping each other" as opposed to criticizing and assessing each other. Jenson found that students who felt uncomfortable gave "step-by-step" procedural answers instead of sharing their reasoning processes on how they solved the problem. Showing respect and caring facilitates positive interactions that lead to the development of a classroom community (Hardin, 2011). How the teacher responds to students matters as well as how students treat each.

At the beginning of the school year, have a conversation with your students about what it means to be part of a learning community that supports each other. You can tell your students that "we are here to support each other to learn math." Ask them, "What does it mean to help each other learn?" Brainstorm ideas and create a class list of ideas. Students need to know that learning math can be a messy process, but through perseverance and sensemaking, math can make sense. Students need to know that it is okay to make mistakes and figure things out! The goal is to create a classroom environment where students feel safe to take risks and share their thinking.

The National Research Council (2019) pointed out that how the student perceives the learning experiences emotionally in the social setting influences the development of the brain. Therefore, creating a positive social environment that supports learning is essential. Emotion, learning, and memory are interconnected (National Research Council, 2019). These interconnections apply to social interactions as well as the learning tasks.

Value Students' Experiences and Home Language

Placing value on informal home language and cultural experiences helps students make connections between their everyday experiences, language, and formal mathematics (National Research Council, 2000). Children should also be encouraged to communicate with their families about the mathematics they are learning, which helps children develop both descriptive language and conventional vocabulary (Whitin & Whitin, 2002).

Use Small Groups/Partners

Small groups are great opportunities for students to express ideas to each other individually. This is much easier to do in a small group. Furthermore, it helps build confidence because students have the time to share out ideas and get feedback before sharing out with the whole group. If a student is stuck or needs some support, he or she can ask a classmate for ideas to get started or help to think through a problem.

Individual think time and small-group discussions are helpful to brainstorm ideas before the whole group discussion. Whole class discussions are much more productive when students have ideas to contribute. Therefore, giving students time to think leads to more productive discussions. This is especially true when students are dealing with more complex problems.

Mixing groups throughout the year helps build classroom community. Examine if your students are productively interacting with each other? Consider reassigning small groups if the group dynamics are not working. The rich ideas that get generated in small-group discussion and individual think time contribute to a more meaningful whole class discussion because students have something to contribute.

PHYSICAL CLASSROOM ROUTINES TO PREPARE FOR WHOLE CLASS DISCUSSIONS

Classroom routines establish expected behaviors that lead to a well-functioning classroom (Hardin, 2011). Consistent and straightforward classroom routines are easier to implement and should be introduced at the beginning of the school year and regularly revisited and refined. One kind of classroom routine is a physical routine. A physical routine is what students physically do to participate in the classroom. This means knowing where to sit, how to get supplies, and what is expected to demonstrate readiness for a discussion.

Watch video 3.1: Subtraction and Grouping Second Grade Lesion Guided Lesson, Introducing a New Concept, from 00:00 min to 1:36 min. The beginning part of the video captures this physical transition.

Shaun Sanchez organized his classroom so that there is space for students to sit on a carpet, either in a configuration of a rectangle or as a group to view the interactive board. He communicates behavior expectations. For example, he walked over to the interactive board and wrote a list of materials for students to gather and bring to the carpet to prepare for the discussion. His list included the following items:

- blocks
- mat
- whiteboard
- marker

"Remember any time we do this, you guys have to be on the dot," reminded Mr. Sanchez. He tells the students, "Your board can be on the blue (blue border of carpet). . . . I would like the whiteboard and the pen behind you." The specific directions on how to organize materials made the transition smooth and fast. There was very little wasted time where the students were off-task. An important point to note is that Mr. Sanchez followed through by making sure his students understood his directions. It was only then he started the lesson.

Classroom Management Routines

- *A signal to indicate transition.* For example, a teacher can ring a bell or say, "Let's get ready for discussion." The teacher needs to *provide clear and explicit instruction* of what this signal means. It may be to sit on the carpet and look at the board for the materials needed.
- *Clear and specific instructions for behavior.* For example, students are expected to sit in a circle with feet crossed and hands on lap.
- *Specific directions with materials.* Students should have the materials they need and know how to get the materials and where to place them. For example, Mr. Sanchez asked students to place the dry erase board behind them so that it did not distract them or clutter the space to work with manipulatives. His instruction also helped students organize their workspace for efficiency.
- *A signal to indicate readiness for discussion.* The teacher's instruction "Show me you are ready" is helpful to get students' attention before engaging in discussion. Getting students' attention focused is helpful for students to listen and participate better. Teacher maintains a respectful atmosphere, the tone of voice, and redirecting behavior.

There are many classroom management books available that address this topic in more detail. Mr. Sanchez pointed out that he practices these routines throughout the school year. Furthermore, he pointed out that he knows his students well and know what they are ready for.

Self-Reflection Question

What physical routines have you established in your class to prepare for whole class discussions?

SOCIAL ROUTINES FOR WHOLE CLASS DISCUSSIONS

Students need to know how to participate in the discussion so that they can explore mathematical problems in the class and dig deeper to develop new insights. How students communicate and interact with each other influences the mathematical understandings, they develop (Boaler, 1997; Hiebert et al., 1997; Schoenfeld, 1998; Boaler & Greeno, 2000). Students must problem-solve, communicate thoughts, listen to alternate views, and reflect on their solutions.

A student who explains the solution to a problem as a series of steps is providing a "calculational" explanation (Yackel & Cobb, 1996). A student who can also justify *how* and *why* something works is thinking at a deeper conceptual level. Both kinds of explanations are necessary in whole class discussions for mathematical learning to take place (Yackel & Cobb, 1996; Star, 2005; Baroody, Feil, & Johnson, 2011). Students not only need to have a rich understanding of how the concepts are interrelated, but they should also understand how to use algorithms accurately to solve problems (Star, 2005; Baroody et al., 2011).

If students' prior math discussion experiences involve mainly describing the steps to solve a problem or performing calculations to get the correct answer (Cobb, Stephan, McClain, & Gravemeijer, 2001), students may initially resist these new expectations. Being asked to explain their reasoning and approaches to solving problems may challenge students' comfort level. Some teachers report that students "don't like to talk." However, their resistance can be overcome when the teacher sets clear expectations that students should prepare for and participate in the discussion.

One teacher reported that when she first started implementing these class discussion strategies, her students' initial test scores slightly dropped. (Her district administered a test that measured student growth during the school year.) However, she continued to apply the strategies described in this book. She discovered at the end of the school year that her students had the highest growth in test scores. Therefore, be patient if students initially resist new expectations and routines. Consistently applying the strategies listed in this book will result in students engaging in productive discussions.

Students do not naturally develop routines for communication. Rather, this is something that you must create with your students. Just like physical routines, students need to learn how to participate in the classroom socially. Before students engage in a discussion, it is important to give them time to think through the problem, use tools, and write out their thinking. By first thinking about a problem and formulating possible solutions, students will be able to support and challenge the thinking of other students.

Posing questions to guide thinking can require students to think more deeply about the problem they are trying to solve. After students have individually thought about the problem, they can work with partners or small group to try out ideas with each other before sharing with the whole class.

Establish expectations of participation in discussions. Students need to know ahead of time that they will be asked to share their thinking with others. This forces students to reflect on the problem more deeply. The following example illustrates how one teacher established expectations.

> Today you are going to get some problems. I would like you to work independently on the problem first. . . . When you are finished, I am going to assign you to work in small groups. Discuss and share your ideas about how to solve the problem. Then we will meet back as a class, and each group will share what they decided. You may solve the problems any way you like.

COMMUNICATING IDEAS SO THAT OTHERS CAN UNDERSTAND

Students need to understand that they are sharing their ideas so that other students can understand their thinking. Writing out problems, or sharing work, is helpful for others to follow thinking. Pointing to what is being discussed is also powerful for focusing the group's attention. Also, students must listen and ask questions if they are unclear about the explanation being presented.

Student explanations must be valued by the group (Bochicchio et al., 2009). Researchers (Bochicchio et al., 2009) point out that students feel comfortable sharing their ideas and opinions with the class only if they feel that their thoughts are valued. Students feel that their thoughts are valued when other students listen to what they are saying and provide constructive feedback on the ideas without criticizing the individual.

Make a distinction between personal criticism and criticism about mathematical ideas. A critique of an idea is not a personal attack. The goal of the conversation is to understand what a student is saying. Therefore, if a student presents an incorrect argument or demonstrates a misconception, the class can view this as a learning opportunity to deepen their understanding of why something does not work.

Explain that disagreements will occur and that students will have different ways of thinking about problems. Students asking higher-level questions can also prompt their critical thinking. For example, you may ask students to justify their answers and explain why one answer works better than another. Provide guidelines on how to respectfully agree or disagree with a student's explanation. For example, students can say, "I agree (disagree) with Scott's strategy because. . . . " Students must justify why they agree or disagree with another student's reasoning. Be clear that they are critiquing ideas and not criticizing individuals.

ACTIVE LISTENING DURING WHOLE CLASS DISCUSSIONS

Active listening is an important part of sense-making in whole class discussions. Students should not passively sit and tune out of the discussion because it is "not their turn to talk." Students should be listening to other students' explanations and thinking about the problem (Yackel, 2003). A teacher can ask students to model what "listening" physically looks like. In the following example, a teacher tells her students what she expects them to do during a discussion:

> Teacher: I have some rules about how we have a conversation. . . . I want each person to talk out and explain their strategy. Every member needs to be listening because I am going to have you explain it later. For example, if I went over to Shawn and asked him how Carmen solved it, then Shawn should be able to tell me the way Carmen explained it. When it comes to your turn, you can say, "I used Samantha's method" or "I used Carmen's method." Or, if you did something different, then you could say, "I used Amber's method, but I did it this way."

The teacher points out her expectations for students to participate in the discussion and communicate their ideas. She asks students to listen to each other's explanations. A student is expected to restate another student's explanation using that student's own words. Students must also connect their explanations with other students' thinking. Having other students contribute to the student's explanation or restating differently can help the class understand the solution or strategy. The teacher establishes a purpose for listening and communicating as a group and models an enthusiasm for mathematical thinking.

Teachers also need to listen to the student explanations to determine what sense the students are making, what they conceptually understand, and what misconceptions they may have (Yackel, 2003). This information is useful in knowing how to facilitate and scaffold the discussion.

Inviting students to restate what another student has said or share a similar or different strategy will force them to compare their strategy with the one being discussed. Students need explicit instruction in routines for active listening and guidelines for acceptable peer interaction. Here are some ideas to get students to listen to each other and share ideas.

Routines for Active Listening and Making New Connections

Strategies for the Classroom: *Routines for Active Listening and Making New Connections*

- Look at and listen to someone who is explaining.
- Ask questions if you don't understand what someone is saying.
- Tell how your explanation is similar or different from other explanations.

- Think about what you are learning about the mathematical concept being discussed.

Self-Reflection Questions

1. What routines do I currently have in place for communication?
2. How effective are these routines support communication?

USING REPRESENTATIONS TO RECORD THINKING

Create, Share, and Explain Representations

When students create a representation to communicate their thinking, other students can visualize what they are saying. Students who are taught to solve problems by using only algorithms in a procedural way may be resistant to drawing pictures and using representations. However, when students learn the algorithm without understanding how and why it works, they have difficulty retaining what they learned. Students can also lack number sense, which is needed to solve problems with algorithms. Students need to learn the "big ideas" of mathematical conceptually and then understand how and why the algorithm works.

Using representations can develop number sense. For example, consider the problem 200 + 250. One student can solve it by adding 200 + 200 to make 400, then adding 50. Another student might recognize that 250 + 250 equals 500, and then subtract 50. Having flexible ways to think about a problem involves developing number sense. Flexibility leads to a deeper understanding of mathematics, and students can use problem-solving strategies if they forget particular steps for an algorithm. Encourage students to use representations to support their thinking.

Self-Reflection Questions

1. How would you encourage students to use a variety of representations such as drawings and manipulatives when solving problems?
2. How do representations help whole class discussions?

CASE STUDY 1: EXAMINING AN UNSUCCESSFUL DISCUSSION

In this case study, a teacher attempts to hold a whole class discussion about division, fractions, and decimals. The discussion is not built around recommended routines that would engage students in thinking about and sharing their ideas. As a result, a full discussion does not take place, and the teacher reverts to showing students step by step how to solve the problem. She concludes in her journal that these students "don't know how to express their ideas about math." As a result, she decides that she needs to "show students several strategies on how to solve problems."

Scenario: The teacher stands in front of the overhead, and the students are seated in rows facing the teacher. The students have their textbooks open to a page on decimals and fractions as well as their homework. The teacher wants her students to think about the relationship between division and fractions so that she can relate it to the concept of decimals. Her specific lesson goal is to show students how to compare fractions by converting them to decimals to figure which one fraction is larger.

TEACHER: What does it mean to divide?

STUDENT: Dividing by an angle?

STUDENT: Decimals and fractions?

Analysis: The teacher starts with a good question with the potential for students to dig deeper to understand the meaning of division. However, she does not begin with a problem that would require students to think about division. The student who responded "decimals and fractions" is likely making a prediction based on the fact that the textbook is open to a page with that lesson title.

TEACHER: Who likes decimals and fractions? Are decimals and fractions the same?

STUDENTS: Yes.

Analysis: Although several students agree that decimals and fractions are the same, they do not explain. This question has also shifted the focus of the original question of "what it means to divide." Now, students are trying to decide "if decimals and fractions are the same" and if they like fractions and decimals.

TEACHER: Let's compare fractions. What's greater? Raise your hands. I want you to think about it. How can we compare two fractions? What is the greater fraction, 3/4 or 6/7?

STUDENT: 6/7.

TEACHER: Okay, I want you to think about it. Raise your hand. How many think 3/4 is greater? Raise your hand if you think 6/7 is greater. How many are not sure? What can we do to compare the two fractions?

Analysis: Although the teacher is asking students to decide if "3/4 is bigger than 6/7," her goal is to help students understand that they can convert the fractions to decimals and then compare the numbers. The focus is on finding the correct answer as opposed to helping students figure out conceptually how to compare fractions. The students still seem to be struggling; the teacher decides to show them how to find the common denominator. She asks students to multiply the numbers as she solves the problem.

TEACHER: Can we write them both as fractions with 28 as a denominator? Could we do that? What is four times six?

STUDENTS: Twenty-four.

TEACHER: What is seven times three?

STUDENTS: Twenty-one.

TEACHER: How does twenty-one compare to twenty-four?

STUDENTS: It is smaller.

TEACHER: So, which fraction is greater?

STUDENTS: 6/7.

Analysis: Students can answer her questions because they involve calculations that they can do. However, it is unclear if they understand why 6/7 is greater, and if they could solve another problem by themselves.

After the teacher demonstrates how to find the common denominator to figure out which fraction is larger, she explains how to compare the quantities by converting the fractions into decimals.

TEACHER: What is the fast way to convert fractions into decimals?

STUDENT: Mentally? Like, 3/4 is 0.75.

TEACHER: What about 6/7? You need a calculator to figure that out.

Analysis: The teacher answers her question of which method she considers more efficient. However, it is unclear if students learned how to compare fractions using a common denominator or by converting to decimals.

Conclusions: Effective discussions require students to be cognitively engaged in sense-making, using their prior knowledge, asking meaningful questions that build on each other, and drawing or making representations to support thinking. One "big idea" of this discussion is to understand what it means to divide and the relationship between decimals and percentage. If we examine the transcript closely, we find that students are not engaged in problem-solving. Students are either guessing at the correct answer or performing calculations to answer the question. There is very little opportunity for students to make connections between these ideas. Students are willing to participate, but classroom routines that support discussion and sense-making seem to be nonexistent.

Self-Reflection Questions

- What suggestions would you give this teacher to get these students to talk?
- What kinds of questions would you have posed if you were the teacher?
- What would you have had as your mathematical goals and objectives for this lesson?

CASE STUDY 2: EXAMINING A SUCCESSFUL DISCUSSION

The teacher in Case Study 1 took part in professional development and worked on improving her discussion. She applied some of the strategies presented in this book and specifically worked on changing her classroom routines for discussion. Case Study 2 takes place a year later. This time, she approaches teaching comparing fraction quantities differently. She starts the lesson by posing a problem for students to solve. Students work individually and share with partners. After students have had a chance to think about this problem, she begins her whole class discussion. Bonnie shares her solution.

BONNIE: 3/4 is bigger than 2/3.

TEACHER: Can you explain to me why you think 3/4 is bigger than 2/3?

BONNIE: Because four is larger than three.

Analysis: The teacher asks students to justify their reasoning for their answers. Even though the student arrived at the correct answer, her reasoning showed that she had a misconception that needed to be addressed.

TEACHER: Does anyone agree with Bonnie?

DREW: 3/4 is bigger than 2/3 because I drew a picture.

TEACHER: Can you draw the picture on the board?

Analysis: Asking the class if they agree with Bonnie's explanation brings students into the discussion; they are expected to listen and think about another student's solution. Drew's picture of two circles divided into thirds and fourths allows the class to visualize the problem and solution.

The teacher focuses the class back on Bonnie's misconception of ignoring the numerator when comparing the fraction quantity. She asks the class if they can rely on only looking at the denominators to make a decision about which fraction is larger. Students conclude that they cannot rely on the denominators alone to tell them which quantity is bigger. When they looked at the model, they observed that a third was bigger than a fourth. However, when they considered the numerators 3/4 was bigger.

> *TEACHER:* So, what else would you do? What is something you were taught to do to compare fractions? Nicole?
>
> *NICOLE:* Find a common denominator.

The student explains how to find the common denominator. Students at this point make a connection between the common denominator and the visual model. Another student raises his hand and comments that he used percentage to figure out his answer. He shares his strategy for comparing fractions.

Conclusion: As you can see, the routines for discussion have changed. Students now provide justifications and representations for their answers and make sense of each other's answers. The teacher activates the student's prior knowledge during the lesson, giving them time to think about the problem ahead of time. Students can agree and disagree respectfully. The level of engagement and participation of students reveals that students understand the math concept, contribute to the discussion, and develop their thinking.

Self-Reflection Questions

1. What kind of routines would you like to establish in your class for students to make their thinking explicit to the group?
2. What is the role of the teacher in helping students make their thinking explicit?
3. How does writing down explanations for the whole group help the discussion?

CHAPTER SUMMARY

Effective whole class discussions require a classroom environment that is nonthreatening and where students are comfortable and feel confident about sharing and critiquing ideas. A positive classroom community needs to be cultivated. Specifically, students need to feel connected to the teacher and each other and treat each other with respect. Physical classroom routines are necessary to prepare for class discussions, followed by social routines that facilitate communication and active listening during the discussion. Routines for communication allow students time to use what they already know, independently think about the problem, share ideas with peers, and then discuss ideas as a class.

Many teachers that I have worked with report that their students are not used to communicating their thinking. Furthermore, they are concerned about finding time to have discussions. However, as these teachers worked on having whole group discussions with their students, they found that their students opened up and were more willing to share ideas. Teachers also commented that students retained what they learned in class discussions. Therefore, they felt that discussions contributed to student learning of mathematics. Most importantly, these teachers found that students became excited about doing the math.

STUDY GUIDE

The following is a suggested sequence of activities designed to help you think about the kinds of physical and social classroom routines needed to facilitate effective whole class discussions. Remember, these routines do not develop immediately. They take time to implement and refine.

IDEAS INTO ACTION

Evaluate Physical and Social Classroom Routines

1. Watch video clips 3.1 and 3.2. Think about how the physical and social classroom routines contribute to discussions in both classrooms. Use the "reflecting on video clips" questions to help you notice routines in the videos.

Teacher

2. Videotape a lesson and observe what kind of physical and social routines are currently in place. Reflect on what is working or not working.

3. Identify areas of strengths and weaknesses.
4. Read "Strategies for Your Classroom" section at the end of the chapter. Identify some strategies that you would like to adapt as part of your classroom routine.
5. Remember, these routines take weeks to implement. Consistently apply them and reflect if these routines are working or not. It may help to videotape your lessons a couple of times and see if you can observe shifts in your teaching. Use the "reflecting on videos" questions to look at your classroom.
6. Think about the kinds of physical and social classroom routines needed for effective whole class discussions. Also, reflect on how to build a supportive classroom community where students feel comfortable to share their ideas and take risks. Video clips from two different classrooms are provided for you to think about how physical and social classrooms contribute to discussions.

Pre-Service Teacher

• If you are not in the classroom yet, think about these ideas and try them out as you student teach or in a practicum setting. Remember, these routines do not develop immediately. They take time to implement and refine. Also, don't try all these strategies out at once either. Pick a few and work on them and keep adding additional strategies.

Reflect and Refine

• As you keep practicing these strategies, use the Reflecting on Your Practice worksheet to think about what you are doing. Use these tools along with the rubrics provided to monitor and adjust your teaching. Consistent expectations and daily practice of routines are needed for these routines to be automatic.

STRATEGIES FOR YOUR CLASSROOM

Routines for Preparing for Discussions

- Think about the problem independently.
- Draw pictures, use manipulatives, or write down the steps you used to help you solve the problem. Be prepared to explain your reasoning.
- Think hard about the problem you are trying to solve.
- Expect to share ideas with others.
- Keep records of thinking in the form of journal or notebook.

Routines for Communicating Thinking So That Others Can Understand

- Use visuals/drawings and models to explain your thinking.
- Explain what the visuals/drawings mean.
- Share and develop ideas with a partner or in a small group.
- Ask other students if they understand your thinking.
- Ask another student to help you if you get stuck.

Routines for Active Listening and Making New Connections

- Look at and listen to someone who is explaining.
- Ask questions if you don't understand what someone is saying.
- Tell how your explanation is similar to or different from other explanations.
- Think about what you are learning about the mathematical concept being discussed.
- Respond to ideas constructively and politely.

Proving or Defending a Position

Use these models and sentence frames to discuss ideas.

- Can you prove your answer?
- I agree with (name), or I disagree with (name).
- My reasoning is similar to/different from yours because. . .
- I think I heard you say . . . Did I say what you meant?
- I'm stuck. Can someone help me?
- This chart shows what I mean.
- This part of my solution is similar to . . . But. . .

Chapter 3

REFLECTING ON PRACTICE

Building a Supportive Classroom Community

1. Do students feel comfortable in the classroom? What can you do to establish mutual respect?

2. How often do you assign students to work with different partners or small groups so that students get the opportunity to know each other?

3. Describe a lesson in which students shared personal experiences and informally used their home language as they developed their understanding of math concepts. What was successful about this lesson? How can you build future lesson plans on this success?

4. What are the strengths and weaknesses of your classroom routines?

5. What changes would you like to make? Why? How will you teach these routines?

REFLECTING ON PRACTICE

Thinking about Physical and Social Routines for Discussion

As you create a math lesson, address the following considerations:

1. What is the math objective of your lesson?

2. What physical routines are needed for this lesson? Describe materials needed, signal to begin a physical routine, and purpose-setting question.

3. Describe how the math objectives can be supported through discussions.

   Individual work:

   Small-group discussion:

   Whole class discussion:

4. Identify how students communicate math in your classroom or a classroom that you are observing. What social routines do students use to participate in the discussion? Evaluate their effectiveness. Can social routines for communication be improved so that all students can participate in discussion and learn the mathematical concepts?

5. Anticipate what kinds of representations may be created during the lesson. Think about how these various kinds of representations can be used for sense-making during the discussion.

6. What are the strengths and weaknesses of how students communicate their ideas in your classroom? Are other students able to understand the explanations? Are routines in place to aid students' communication?

REFLECTING ON PRACTICE

Routines for Listening

1. What do your students do to listen to the class conversation? Are they engaged in the conversation? Are they able to follow other students' explanations and think about their explanations? Is there a purpose for students to listen?

2. What are the strengths and weaknesses of your current classroom routines?

3. What would you modify? Why?

4. Describe the kinds of communication that take place during a classroom discussion.

- Is it a group conversation in which the whole class is engaged in the discussion?
- Is the conversation between only the teacher and student?
- Are all students participating in the discussion or only a few students participating?

STUDENT SELF-EVALUATION RUBRIC

Name_____

Table 3.1   Student Self-Evaluation Rubric

I prepared for the discussion by thinking about the problem, solving problem, and drawing/writing down my ideas.	*I communicated my ideas clearly by using representations when needed.*	*I listened to the discussion and asked questions when confused.*	*I analyzed other students' ideas.*

CLASS PARTICIPATION RUBRIC FOR DISCUSSION

Date:_____ Title_____

Table 3.2   Class Participation Rubric

Student name	*Preparing for discussion *draw picture*	*Presenting ideas so that others can understand *using representation*	*Listening (includes asking questions if confused)*	*Analyzing ideas presented*

Chapter 4

Optimize Learning through Planning

We understand something if we see how it is related or connected to other things we know.

(Hiebert, 2003, emphasis added)

Planning is critical for making targeted teaching decisions to support student learning. The goal is to "work smarter, not harder." Therefore, when you plan carefully, you can optimize how you use class time to support student learning. Planning affects the pacing of lessons.

FIRST LEVEL OF PLANNING: IDENTIFY CONCEPTS AND SKILLS

The *first level of planning* involves identifying long-term goals to figure out what math content students need to learn during the school year. Standards and curriculum scope and sequence documents outline what students need to know. Once long-term goals are identified, it is helpful to look at the curriculum and see how the topics are organized/sequenced for the academic year. The table of contents provides an outline of the topics covered and the sequence in which it is organized. Figuring out how the standards are connected to the curriculum is helpful.

The math content students need to learn involves a combination of *conceptual* and *procedural* knowledge. Understanding the difference between *conceptual knowledge* and *procedural knowledge* is important for figuring out the concepts and skills students need to learn. *Conceptual knowledge* refers to *what* students need to *understand* mathematically, whereas *procedural knowledge* involves the steps students take to solve a problem.

45

What Does It Mean to Understand a Concept?

Understanding a math concept involves assimilating several layers of interconnected meaning. For example, consider the part-whole concept of ½ as illustrated in figure 4.1. Just because a student memorizes that the written symbol ½ can be read as "one-half" does not mean the student understands the concept of ½. For example, ½ can represent part of a whole such as a pie cut into two pieces. One of the pieces represents one part of the two equal pieces of the whole pizza.

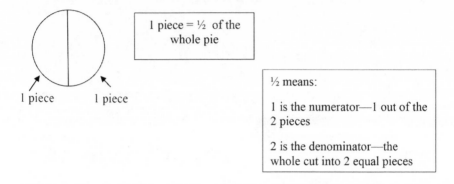

Some students may view ½ as one piece of the pie and visualize it as a single unit. However, students can make the connection that ½ represents a fraction only when they make the connection that it is part of the whole unit—the 1 represents the numerator, and the 2 represents the denominator. The numerator represents one piece of the pie that has been cut into two equal pieces.

The ½ can also be viewed as a division relationship when the whole is being equally divided between two people. In this situation, the ½ represents a fair sharing situation. Furthermore, students must also understand the concept of equivalency (equal-sized pieces). This requires understanding where to physically cut (partition) the pie so that it yields two equal-sized pieces.

Students not only need to understand mathematical concepts, but they also need to understand *how* to use procedures to appropriately solve problems. When students understand *why* a procedure works, they are also more likely to remember and use the procedure properly in different situations.

What Is Procedural Knowledge?

Procedural knowledge refers to what students should be able *to do* to solve the problem. It involves knowing "the steps" to solve the problem such as adding fractions with common denominators. For example, students can add ½ + ½ by adding the numerators together because this problem has the common denominator of 2. Just because a student knows "the steps" to solve the problem does not mean that the student naturally understands *why* these procedures work.

The student could have simply memorized a rule. The problem of memorizing a rule without understanding *why* it works is that it limits *transfer*. In other words, a student may have difficulty knowing when to use a rule in a novel situation. Furthermore, students tend to forget rules when they do not make sense to them. Therefore, the combination of conceptual and procedural knowledge allows students to be more successful in solving problems and learning math.

USING A CONCEPT MAP TO EXPLORE CONNECTIONS

Creating a concept map is an easy way to explore what needs to be taught. A concept map (Novak & Cañas, 2006) is a useful graphic tool for identifying key relationships and connections between mathematical concepts and ideas. In a concept map, information is organized in connected boxes or circles to indicate hierarchical relationships of ideas as illustrated in figure 4.2. The "big ideas" are the guiding principles of what students should learn; the sub-concepts are usually the short-term goals in lessons that lead up to the development of the larger goals and concepts.

Mathematics Standards such as the Common Core Standards for Mathematical Practice (CCSSM, 2010) and math curriculum scope and sequence outline concepts and skills that students should learn. For example, fourth-grade teachers who were part of the Nevada Mathematics Project created the following concept

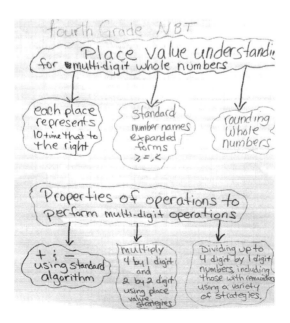

Figure 4.2. Concept Map Created by Teachers

map. They examined the fourth-grade Number and Operations Standards in the Common Core Standards for Mathematical Practice (CCSSM, 2010).

The Common Core Standards list the "big mathematical ideas" and breaks them down into smaller sub-concepts. An overarching grade 4 standard is "Use place value understanding and properties of operations to perform multi-digit arithmetic." This goal is broken down into these standards:

4.NBT.4. Fluently add and subtract multi-digit whole numbers using the standard algorithm.

4.NBT.5. Multiply a whole number of up to four digits by a one-digit whole number, and multiply two two-digit numbers, using strategies based on place value and the properties of operations. Illustrate and explain the calculation by using equations, rectangular arrays, and area models.

The "big idea" that students need to understand is the concept of place value and properties of operations. The sub-concept covers properties of addition (e.g., if zero is added to a number, the number will remain the same; if two whole numbers are added, the quantity increases). Teachers found it helpful to study the standards and then create a concept map as illustrated before (see Figure 4.2) to make sense of the standards and see connections. Ultimately, a teacher is responsible for helping students learn math as outlined in state and district standards.

Understanding what needs to be taught in the standards and curriculum will make teaching a lot less stressful and more effective. Look at the *Table of Contents* in the curriculum to examine how the topics are organized, and think about the sequence of topics about the standards. This action allows you to make a connection between standards and curriculum and think about the pacing of lessons. I have also developed a website, http://www.mathdiscussions.wordpress.com, which has tons of resources and links to help you make sense of the Common Core Standards for Mathematical Practice. (Go through the Lesson Planning Tab.)

Good teaching involves adapting your lessons to students' needs. Therefore, concept maps are helpful to know what to assess to drive your teaching decisions. This means you must be flexible with your lesson plans to adapt to students' needs.

EXAMINE PROGRESSION OF CONCEPTS ACROSS GRADES

Understanding how math concepts progress across the grades is helpful. This way you can identify gaps in students' prior knowledge. Also, you can figure out how to scaffold or extend students' thinking if it needs to be challenged further. Teachers in the Nevada Math Project gathered in grade-level teams and identified the "big ideas" that the students should know. Each grade-level team presented what is covered in their grade level, and then the whole group examined how the concepts developed across the grades. A sample is illustrated in Figure 4.3.

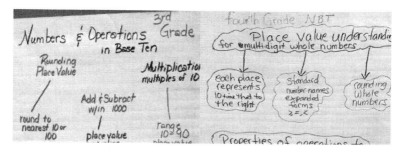

Figure 4.3.　Progression of Mathematics Standards

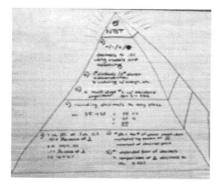

Figure 4.4.　Teachers Explore the Progression of Standards

The teachers when examining the chart paper posters noticed how the concept of place value was extended each year. Many teachers find it helpful to think about the standards before the start of the school year due to lack of time when teaching. Look at the grade level above and below the grade level you teach. This way, you will have a sense of what prior knowledge students should have, and you can support any gaps in their learning. Also, you will know how to extend grade-level content or challenge students further. Each grade level is a building block for the next grade level.

Sequencing Lessons

Planning math lessons and thinking about sequencing help teachers anticipate the path their students might follow to learn the math concept. Therefore, planning a week at a time is helpful because you can lay out a possible learning path for students. A *unit plan* tool is provided for you at the end of

Table 4.1 Unit Plan Example

Lesson	Math Concept	Standard	Skills	Problem to Pose	Anticipated Errors/ Misconceptions
1	Part to whole and decomposing fractions Benchmark fractions	5.NF.A2	Represent a fraction Decompose a fraction, add/ subtract with like denominators, use benchmark fractions		Vocabulary difficulties Benchmark fractions used incorrectly Numerator vs. denominator roles
2	Equivalent fractions	5.NF.A1	Identify and create equivalent fractions Use several strategies and justify answers.	½ is equivalent to? Show why 2/3 is equivalent to using a model.	Not multiplying the numerator and denominator by the same amount Calculation errors
3	Comparing fractions with like and unlike denominators	5.NF.A1 5.NF.A2	Use benchmark fractions correctly. Find common multiples and create equivalent fractions.	Greater than or less than with fractions, sequenced from like to unlike denominators Order fractions.	Incorrect multiples, not ordering correctly because of trouble finding common denominators
4	Adding fractions with unlike denominators	5.NF.A.1	Finding common denominators Adding fractions	2/3 + 1/2 with numbers getting more difficult	Adding the denominator Incorrect common denominators
5	Subtracting fractions with unlike denominators	5.NF.A.1	Finding common denominators Subtracting fractions	2/3 − 1/2 with numbers getting more difficult	Subtracting the denominator Incorrect common denominators

the chapter. Specifically, examine the topics for the week and how they are sequenced. Also, identify a problem to pose and think about errors and misconceptions students might have and how these lessons connect to standards. The goal of planning for the week is to understand the topic that will be taught as it relates to the math unit in the curriculum.

Lessons should be carefully sequenced to optimize learning. Sequencing lessons so that the math concepts build on each other is critical for supporting student learning. However, these plans must be flexible so that they can be adapted to support student understanding. Making targeted instructional decisions is much easier if you know where you are headed. Supporting students to learn involves building on their prior knowledge by helping them make new connections. This contrasts with simply reading the math textbook like a cookbook recipe and following it step by step without reflection.

If you modify curricula or supplement your existing curricula, *make sure you pay attention to how lessons are sequenced* so that the mathematical concepts build on each other in a logical progression. Not sequencing curricula or teaching random lessons without thinking about how they connect and build on each other leads to ineffective teaching and discussions. The goal is to help students make meaningful mathematical connections to optimize learning.

How time is used within a lesson is important. Think about how you use your instruction time. What kinds of typical routines take place? How do you use your class time? Sometimes these teaching routines become invisible because they have become automatic routines and you no longer think about them. Reflect on what a typical lesson looks like in your classroom. An effective lesson has the following components:

- time to go over homework problems that students did not understand
- time for problem-solving and thinking
- time to share with partner/small group
- time for whole class discussion to share ideas, clarify misconceptions and errors, and make new mathematical connections
- opportunities for the teacher to informally assess student reasoning.

The following 5E lesson format, adapted from Roger Bybee (1997), is helpful for teaching lessons through problem-solving and sense-making. This is just one way to think about how to structure time. Use a format that works for you. Teachers have found that using the following structure provides the opportunity to support students to engage in problem-solving and discussion.

- Check homework quickly by against an answer key. Discuss any problems that students might have struggled with. Perhaps that could be a focus of discussion. Typically, homework should be assigned when students are confident in solving the problems, and it is just practice.

- The goal is not to take 20–30 minutes of class instruction time checking homework. It should be noted that it might be more efficient to assign online homework where students get instantaneous feedback and helpful hints on what they did wrong. If your district has adopted such a curriculum, then class time does not need to be spent checking homework. Rather, you can spend time addressing issues that came up that students had difficulty understanding.

The Lesson

- Teacher poses a problem for students to solve.
- Students think about the problem individually and work with partner/small group to come up with a solution.
- The whole class discussion takes place. Big mathematical ideas are explicit so that the knowledge can be used as tools to solve additional problems.
- Students solve additional problems using what they just learned; perhaps some problems might have some challenge to it that will extend their knowledge.
- Teacher identifies issues that came up as they solved the problems to extend thinking through discussion as time permits. Exit ticket/assess student understanding.

The goals and purpose must drive the format of lessons as opposed to following a formulaic approach. Sometimes, there may be time students need to practice; other times they may need a more guided lesson. When students are introduced to new concepts, they engage in problem-solving activities that challenge their thinking so that they can learn new information.

THE 5E ADAPTED LESSON PLAN FORMAT

1. Engage: *The teacher poses an interesting question or problem that captures students' attention, activates their prior knowledge, and leads students to begin thinking about the concept.* The problem should address the mathematics that students will learn in the lesson. An appropriate problem has the right level of cognitive demand (challenge) so that it requires thinking and problem-solving (Smith, Bill, & Hughes, 2008). Therefore, the problem must

- build on students' prior knowledge
- engage students' interest
- align with the mathematical goals of the lesson
- require students to engage in thinking, not just repeat a procedure
- allow for multiple ways that it can be solved using a variety of representations
- help students deepen their understanding of mathematics
- connect to the mathematical goals of the lesson

A problem that is too easy and requires minimal thinking is not a good one for discussion. There would be nothing to talk about. Similarly, a problem that is too hard where students don't have an entry point to figure out how to solve it is also not a good choice. The Engage phase should take no more than 5 to 10 minutes, and specifically introduce the main concept of the lesson.

2. Explore: After a problem has been posted for students to solve, they should have time to individually reflect on it. Opportunities to discuss ideas with a partner or small group help think about the problem. This helps students think through the problem by bouncing ideas off each other. Students can use tools and create representations to help them problem-solve. These become tools for thinking and communicating ideas.

When students are working, the teacher should formatively assess student thinking and understanding. This process involves observing the types of student strategies and reasoning, errors, and misconceptions that are taking place. The teacher tries to figure out what the students understand mathematically and can do. For example, a pre-service teacher was observing a student figure out whether 39 connector cubes or 41 connector cubes were bigger. She journaled the following:

> *My student was unable to tell which pile had more. At first, he began counting with one-to-one tagging/correspondence but could not keep track. I asked him if there was another way he could keep track of his counting. He then started grouping them into stacks of 5 to count faster and keep track. When he completed both, I asked him if there was another way to count the connector cubes faster. Asking sense-making questions like this help students work through and explain their thinking (Lamberg, pg.116, 2013). He then said he could count by tens, which is what I wanted him to realize. After he did this, I had him convert them into a table of counting the number of tens and ones in the problem. Miles visually realized 41 only had four tens, and 39 only had three tens.*
> —Sydney Heaivilin

The teacher can gain a deeper understanding of thinking by posing questions to clarify student thinking. Knowing what to look for is helpful when assessing student reasoning. Teachers can use classroom experiences and also draw from research to recognize possible ways students are thinking about the problem. Researchers on professional noticing point out that noticing ways student reason does not naturally happen (Jacobs, Lamb, & Phillip, 2010). Therefore, anticipating what students might do helps notice student reasoning.

As the teacher walks around and observes student thinking, the teacher should be making a mental note of the learning that is taking place and should think about the next instructional move. This means that formative assessment alone is not enough. The teacher needs to think about what to do with the information. Some teachers found that having a clipboard helps make any notes while walking around.

If the problem that you gave is too difficult for students, you may want to provide a simpler problem or explore a simpler problem that might help them solve a more complex problem. Perhaps, they are all successful in solving the problem. Then a discussion is not warranted about that problem; you may want to decide what to do next to challenge their thinking, what problem to pose, or how to extend what they already know.

Note: There are times when new information is introduced. When this is the case, solving one rich problem and discussing it can be powerful. However, if students have discussed a rich problem and they are practicing using what they already know, it may make sense for students to solve multiple problems to practice what they learned. During this time, the teacher can walk around and observe what the students can do and discuss any problems or issues that arise that they may have difficulty with.

3. Explain: After students have explored a problem, a whole class discussion can take place. The purpose of a whole class discussion is for students to explore the underlying mathematics by sharing their reasoning, uncovering errors and misconceptions to make sense of the mathematics. Chapter 6 elaborates on how a teacher can facilitate deeper mathematical thinking and connections by using the *three levels of sense-making framework*.

4. Elaborate: Once a discussion has taken place and the "big mathematical ideas" are made explicit, the teacher can pose a question to extend thinking by introducing new information to build and extend student thinking. For example, students discussed whether 41 or 39 built with unfixed cubes were bigger. The teacher could extend student thinking by introducing a place value mat to organize their manipulatives and scaffold how to write the numbers.

5. Evaluate: In the final phase of the instructional model, the teacher can provide an exit ticket problem or a journal entry problem to assess what the student can figure out independently. For example, the teacher could pose another problem such as 45 and 56 to see if the students could independently figure out which number is bigger. The evaluation allows the teacher to gauge what students understood and what can be refined. *Note*: Practice is an integral part of learning math and making sure that students retain what they learn:

Checklists are powerful tools to keep track of individual and class thinking. The following is an example of a checklist. The teacher could look at the exit ticket and make a check mark by what the student understood. This allows for keeping track of individual student thinking and progress while simultaneously giving a quick snapshot of how the class is progressing. The following is an example of a checklist created by teachers. The concept map is a great tool to turn into a checklist.

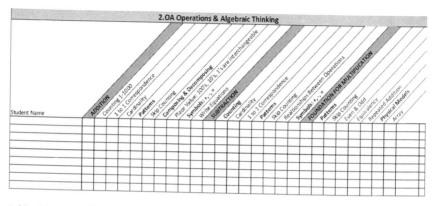

Table 4.2   Sample Formative Assessment Checklist

Examples of students' solutions to two problems involving fractions are presented at the end of this chapter. Take a look at student's solutions and think about how you might use this information to support student learning. How would you sequence a whole class discussion and why?

CHAPTER SUMMARY

There are three levels of planning that lead to effective whole class discussions. This chapter discussed the first two levels. The first level of planning involves identifying long- and short-term goals about what students need to know conceptually and procedurally. Once mathematical goals are identified, it helps to connect these goals to the curriculum and think about sequencing and lesson planning for the week. The second level of planning involves thinking about the lesson. This includes how time is used and deciding what problem to pose and lesson to implement.

STUDY GUIDE

Strategies for Your Classroom

Three Levels of Planning

First Level: Identify Long-Term and Short-Term Goals and Interconnections

- Identify long-term and short-term mathematical goals.
- Identify the concepts students should understand and what procedures they should be able to do.
- Develop a concept map to see how these topics are connected.

Second Level: Plan the Individual Lesson

- Plan the lesson with the discussion in mind.
- Select tasks that support mathematical goals and engage students in reasoning and problem-solving.
- Anticipate what students might do and possible topics for discussion.

Third Level: During the Lesson, Choose a Topic or Problem for Discussion Based on Student Reasoning and Sense-Making

- Identify student reasoning, misconceptions, errors, and tasks.
- Identify a topic for discussion.
- Address short-term and long-term goals.
- Sequence the discussion to build students' understanding.

FIRST-LEVEL PLANNING

Look at your state standards/district standards and identify the "big mathematical ideas" that you want students to understand for your grade level. It helps to look at a grade level above and below.

Create Concept Map

- Create a concept map or list of key ideas and sub-ideas that students need to know.
- Look at a grade level above and below and create a concept map for each grade level.
- Ask yourself: "What do my students need to know at my grade level?"
- If you are unsure what the standards mean, there are several resources on the web. A math methods textbook can be helpful as well to look at the research.
- http://www.mathdiscussions.wordpress.com

Modification Ideas for Teacher Professional Development Session:
Each grade-level team can create a concept map for the grade level they teach. The groups can share and analyze each other's concept maps to see how the math concepts build across the grade level.

Examine Curriculum

- Look at the Table of Contents of the Math Curriculum to evaluate the scope and sequence for the school year.

- Ask yourself, "How are the topics laid out and how does it relate to the standards."
- Where do topics intersect?
- What materials and resources are provided for you to support student learning?

Create Unit Plan

Use the "Rubric for Unit Plan" provided, or create your own. The unit plan provides you with a road map to lay out the lessons for the week. Specifically, look at what topics you are covering and how these build on each other. The *unit plan* helps you anticipate what students might do and allows you to quickly see the big picture.

RUBRIC FOR UNIT PLAN

Mathematics Topic: _____

Table 4.2 Sample Formative Assessment Checklist

Lesson	Math Concept (Big Ideas) (Sub-concepts)	Standard	Skills	Problem to Pose	Anticipated Student Errors, Misconceptions, Pre-conceptions
1					
2					
3					
4					
5					

CASE STUDY: TEACHER INTERVIEWS

Watch the classroom videos and teacher interviews presented in this book and think about how these teachers thought about planning. *Watch Video 4.1: Teacher Interview-Second Grade*

Reflection Questions:

1. How does Mr. Sanchez plan out his lesson?
2. How does Mr. Sanchez think about sequencing?
3. What kind of scaffolds does Mr. Sanchez think about?

Mr. Sanchez explained that they are going to start with mental math and they are working with the addition with regrouping. His goal is to have his students figure out which strategy is most efficient. Then they will wrap up the two-digit addition with regrouping and move on to subtraction. The students had been working on building subtraction with the base 10 blocks.

Now, they are going to work on writing the subtraction problem in expanded form so that they can work with regrouping. He viewed this part of the lesson as a more guided lesson because he wanted students to understand a specific strategy. Mr. Sanchez's interview illustrates how he planned his lesson by building on students' prior knowledge, having them engage in problem-solving, and introducing a new concept through "guided intervention." He also thought about the tools to use to support student thinking.

TEACHER INTERVIEW

Watch video 4.1: Fifth-Grade Teacher Interview

Reflection Questions:

1. What are some key things Mrs. Sanchez thought about when planning her lesson?
2. What did she consider when planning her lesson?

Ana Sanchez explained that when she taught her lesson (see video clip 4.1), she carefully selected the problem in her lesson because it cut across several grade spans so that everyone could have access to the problem. She explained that "even though all students are not an expert, they should know enough to get started, and also the students who are more experts can focus on the complex issues." She further added that "even those students need to slow down and explain their thinking."

The teacher interviews provide insight into the thinking processes that these teachers engaged with to teach the lesson.

Lesson Planning: Level II Guideline

Lesson Objective: What math concept do you want students to learn and what skills do they need to develop?
Standard: What standards are you addressing?
Prior Knowledge: What background knowledge is needed for the lesson?
Materials Needed: What materials are needed for your lesson?

Lesson

1. **Engage:** The teacher poses an interesting question or problem that captures students' attention, activates their prior knowledge, and leads students to begin thinking about the concept.
Note: The problem should address the mathematics that students will learn in the lesson. An appropriate problem has the right level of cognitive demand (challenge) so that it requires thinking and problem-solving.

Therefore, the problem must:

- require students to engage in thinking, not just repeat a procedure
- allow for multiple ways that it can be solved using a variety of representations
- help students deepen their understanding of mathematics
- engage students' interest.

Include in Lesson Plan:

- What problem you are going to pose?
- What key mathematical ideas will come out of this problem?
- What questions would you pose to get students to start thinking?
- What will you assess with regard to student reasoning?. Write out some strategies, and misconceptions children might have. (The purpose of writing this part down is to anticipate what students might do and that you might look for.)

Explore: After a problem has been posed for students to solve, they should have time to individually reflect on it and then discuss their ideas with a partner or small group.

When students are working, the teacher should walk around and listen to conversations. Look at student work and pose questions. The goal is to figure out what kind of reasoning strategies that are emerging. What are they understanding and what are they confused about? During this time, you will be planning your next instructional move.

Interpreting student work and conversations as they related to the concept map that you had created is helpful. What are they understanding and not understanding mathematically? What underlying mathematics or reasoning strategies should you address? Is the problem too easy or difficult? Should you scaffold their thinking?

Note: Students could solve multiple problems if they are waiting for some students to finish their problem. This way, the students have something to work on and challenge their thinking.

Include in Lesson Plan: A problem or list of problems for students to solve.

Explain: This is the whole class discussion

After they have explored a problem, students meet to explain their reasoning. Discussion leads students to recognize patterns and concepts and describe them in their own words. Students also begin to see errors and misconceptions that may have led them to an incorrect solution. The discussion must also be based on the teacher's assessment of student thinking and work to have students explain and elaborate on their thinking.

What to include in the lesson plan – What are some possible topics for discussion? What errors or misconceptions might come up? How might you sequence the discussion? What would be a low level to a more sophisticated strategy?

Elaborate: How might students' thinking be extended? (This is the third level of sense-making.) What question or connection can be made to extend students' thinking?

Assess: Administer an Exit Ticket. Provide each student with an opportunity to solve a problem independently to assess what they learned. This information is useful to plan the next day's lesson.

REFLECTING ON LESSON PLAN FORMATS

Please note that every lesson plan should not follow a rigid format. The format should be adjusted based on the goals of the lesson and the context. Mrs. Sanchez focused on a rich problem for the entire lesson. Therefore, her lesson was broken into posing the problem, having students try it out, scaffolding student thinking through discussion and solving a simpler problem, students working on the problem again, and students discussing the solution. Her lesson focused on helping students use problem-solving skills to a real-world context to use division that results in a decimal answer that they had learned.

Mr. Sanchez broke up the lesson into three segments. His class were second-grade students, and varying the activities kept them engaged. The first part involved a review related to the calendar. Mr. Sanchez activated students' prior knowledge by asking them to think about the distance from 60 to 100. He asked, "How many do I need to add to get to 100?" He had provided students with a visual tool that included a 100 chart and a place value mat on the interactive board. Students could mentally visualize these tools to solve the addition problem.

If students are still learning a new concept or tackling a complex multi-step problem, they need more scaffolding and time to think through the problem as opposed to doing the problems using mental strategies. This can be accomplished by giving students individual reflection time and time to share ideas with a partner or small group and then discussion group.

You can see an example of greater scaffolding in part II of Mr. Sanchez's lesson that involved introducing subtraction with regrouping. The main goal of the lesson for that day was to help students build two-digit subtraction problems with blocks. He wanted students to be able to break the numbers apart to regroup and write it in expanded form. For example, the number 56 can be split apart as 40 +16 which is made up of 4 tens and 16 ones. A whole class discussion can have different goals. Nevertheless, an important part is for students is to engage in sense-making and communicate ideas.

Teachers should provide students "guided intervention" (Gravemeijer & van Galen, 2003) because students don't necessarily "discover" efficient strategies or develop deeper mathematical understandings on their own. Therefore, class time must be efficiently used to guide students to make mathematical connections.

Chapter 5

Third Level of Planning: What Do We Talk About?

A well-planned whole class discussion efficiently uses class time to support the learning of *all* students. Learning happens when students make connections between what they already know and new information (National Research Council, 2000). A mathematical discussion must be thought of as a conversation that takes place over time. Learning happens when students make mathematical connections *within* and *across* lessons. The teacher decides what to talk about based on mathematical goals and student reasoning as illustrated in Figure 5.1.

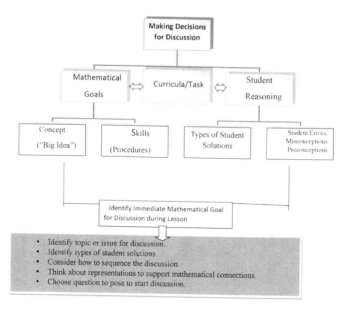

Figure 5.1. **The Decision Making Process for Discussion**

Deciding what to talk about is a complex decision. The different levels of planning discussed in previous chapters help you figure out the focus of the discussion. Formative assessment should drive the decision-making process of the whole class discussion. Students can make stronger mathematical connections more efficiently if the discussion is well planned and students can follow along.

Over 100 teachers from the Nevada Math Project brought student work from their classrooms to a professional development session. The teachers sorted their student responses by types of solutions that emerged in the lesson. We discovered that there were two to five different ways that students were thinking about the problem regardless of the lesson or grade level taught. Teachers were relieved to know that they did not have to address 30 different ways of thinking; rather, they could address the kinds of thinking that emerge in a lesson. This makes teaching a whole lot less stressful.

Claudia Bertolone-Smith and Linda Koyen wrote an article in *Teaching Children Mathematics* on what they did as teachers to facilitate discussions. One of the strategies that they liked to use was "call for answers" (Bertolone-Smith & Gillette-Koyen, 2019). They recorded all the possible answers on the board, and students defended a specific answer. Through discussion, they were able to eliminate answers that did not make sense. This simple act of recording the different responses on the board allows the teacher to assess class thinking quickly, and it helps clear up any errors in thinking as well.

It is helpful to think about students' reasoning strategies and how it relates to the mathematical goals of the lesson when evaluating student reasoning. Simply figuring out reasoning strategies is not enough. Figuring out the next instructional move to help thinking forward is a critical part of teaching so that learning can happen.

ANALYZING STUDENT WORK TO PLAN DISCUSSION

The examples in figures 5.2–5.4 illustrate how a group of teachers evaluated student responses to a problem and categorized their responses. They reflected on the kind of support or scaffolding each type of solution needed to move thinking forward.

3. (6.EE.6 and 6.EE.7) Jim removed 27 gallons of water from a rainwater storage tank. There are 59 gallons left in the tank. Write and solve an equation Jim can use to find out how much water was in the tank earlier.

What we Learned About Student Thinking/Learning	Recommendations for Adapting and Modifying Teaching
These students can process this as a single step word problem but use the incorrect operation to solve. These students are unable to write an equation to match the given real-world situation.	Have these students go back and re-read what the problem is asking (read for understanding) and see which operation would make sense in this scenario.

3. (6.EE.6 and 6.EE.7) Jim removed 27 gallons of water from a rainwater storage tank. There are 59 gallons left in the tank. Write and solve an equation Jim can use to find out how much water was in the tank earlier.

What we Learned About Student Thinking/Learning	Recommendations for Adapting and/or Modifying Teaching
These students can process this as a single step word problem. These students were unable to write an algebraic equation to match the given real-world situation. These students used the correct operation to solve.	With these students, spend time revisiting how to write an equation and to read carefully to determine what is being asked of them in the problem. These students still need help in creating an equation to match a real-world situation using a variable.

3. (6.EE.6 and 6.EE.7) Jim removed 27 gallons of water from a rainwater storage tank. There are 59 gallons left in the tank. Write and solve an equation Jim can use to find out how much water was in the tank earlier.

What we Learned About Student Thinking/Learning	Recommendations for Adapting and/or Modifying Teaching
These students can write an equation to match the given real-world scenario. These students use the inverse operation to solve the problem. These students solve the problem like a traditional one-step subtraction problem and do not show keeping the equation balanced by performing the same operation on each side of the equal sign.	These students can work on explaining their answer in terms of the context of the problem. Example: There was 86 gallons of water in the storage tank.

Once solutions are analyzed, the teacher must decide how to sequence the discussion so that students can make sense of what is being shared. Look at the student work above and think about how you would sequence the whole class discussion. What points would you like to highlight?

Van Zoest et al. (2017) suggested that the following issues can lead to great discussions where you can help extend student learning and make mathematical connections. These include:

1. *Extending*—Help students think about mathematics beyond the lesson. (Challenge them to think deeper.)
2. *Incorrect mathematics*—If students are making incorrect errors, the discussion becomes an opportunity to clear up any misconceptions. Students can think about why the errors they are making does not make sense and what they should do about it.
3. *Sense-making*—Explore underlying mathematical concepts related to the problem they are solving. This way they can transfer their new learning to other problems.
4. *Contradiction*—Student responses have competing interpretations or conflict with one another in some way.
5. *Mathematical confusion*—Students are confused about the math. Discussion can clear up any confusion.

Using models and visuals is a powerful way to start the conversation. This gets everyone on the same page and gives students an entry point. Therefore, using problems that have a visual drawing or numbers that model the situation is a great place to start. The teacher's questions can get at having students explain how the numbers in the problem relate to the problem context.

When looking at the analysis of student work in the examples in figures 5.2–5.4, the issue that needs to be addressed is how to help students connect the numbers in the problem to the problem context and write an equation using the correct operation. The goal is not to get everyone in the class to share, rather make sense of the kinds of thinking that emerged in the class to make sense of the mathematics and problem-solving strategies.

Watch video clip 5.1, Fifth-Grade Problem-Solving Lesson (Division/ Decimals). Video length: 30 minutes https://textbooks.rowman.com/lamberg

Note: This video presents the lesson and includes Mrs. Sanchez reflecting throughout the lesson. These reflections provide insight into her decision-making process. The teacher interview video clip reveals that Mrs. Sanchez carefully planned the lesson to include a rich problem. This problem selected tied together their prior learning and served as a bridge for future lessons.

Also, she thought about how to organize her class for collaboration and helping them engage in sense-making.

Not only did Mrs. Sanchez think about the mathematics from the lesson but also the kinds of problem-solving she wanted to emerge from the task lesson. She chose this problem because she felt that students at all levels could have an entry point. She explained that it covers three grade-level content standards. She carefully had students sit in heterogeneous groups so that they could help each other and engage in divergent thinking to solve the problem.

MATH FORUM PROBLEM OF THE WEEK

Building the Fence Problem #3031 (NCTM Problem of the Week)

Herta wants to build a picket fence in her front yard. Her design has fence posts that are 8.5 feet apart, with 19 pickets between each set of posts.

Question: If the pickets are 3 inches wide, how wide should the gaps be so that everything is evenly spaced?

Lesson Goals

Mrs. Sanchez explained that her students are used to having a problem of the week every Friday. She expected the problem to take about an hour to 90 minutes.

Mrs. Sanchez: It is built on team collaboration. And they are getting to the point where we see different strategies. I am focusing more on: Are they using a model strategy? Are they using an algorithm? Are they looking at the question? Most of the students just tend to pull numbers from word problems, so I just strategically place this problem for them not to just pull the numbers so that they just don't work.

Mrs. Sanchez *anticipated* what students might do. During the lesson, she *monitored* what the students were doing and made decisions on having student share answers. Margaret Smith and Mary Kay Stein wrote a book titled *5 Practices for Orchestrating Productive Mathematics Discussions* (2011). In this book, she outlines five practices that include *anticipating, monitoring, sequencing, selecting,* and *connecting.* Mrs. Sanchez's lesson incorporated these practices as part of her teaching.

The Lesson

• *Introduction—Pose Problem*

Mrs. Sanchez introduced the problem to the students by having students read the problem out loud together. "If the pickets are 3 inches wide. How wide should the gap be if things are evenly spaced?" Mrs. Sanchez pointed out that they see fences all the time, and they see that the pickets are pretty even. The students were given a rubric to help them solve the problem. They discussed how to use the strategies outlined in the rubric. For example, Mrs. Sanchez asked students to try more than two strategies; she pointed out the algorithm and model.

Students worked collaboratively in small groups to solve the problem for 10 minutes, while the teacher walked around, observed, and listened to student thinking and posed clarifying questions. By doing this, Mrs. Sanchez knew exactly what each group was doing and thinking as revealed by the following interview:

- *Teacher Reflection: Formative Assessment of Group Thinking*

  Mrs. Sanchez: One group has the right thinking, and they are totally on track . . . the other groups are revising and rethinking. I have two groups who are struggling to get started. And, in a moment, I am going to give them a hint and not go to the group that has the answer.

  This assessment allowed Mrs. Sanchez to plan her next instructional move.

- *Whole Class Discussion—Check in Progress*

Students continued to work through the problem in groups. Mrs. Sanchez decided to scaffold their thinking by building on their current thinking. She asks the class to share their answers, and four different solutions are recorded on the board. Note that out of several groups there were four different ways the class was thinking about the problem.

One student explains that he thought about the problem as 8.5 divided by 3 inches. Mrs. Sanchez asked him what the numbers meant and labeled his division problem on the board. The student explained that the 3 represents the inches and the 8.5 represents the distance of the fence. Mrs. Sanchez uses gestures as she asks for clarification.

Another student explains that she thought about the problem as 19 divided by 3. The 19 represented the pickets that are divided by 3 inches. The teacher writes pickets and inches under the numbers. This makes the units explicit to the whole class. The teacher asks the class if that way of thinking about the problem would help them. The students answer "no."

TEACHER: If we were to do that, it would be?

STUDENT: 6 1/3

TEACHER: 6 and a 1/3, that would not help us.

Then the teacher asks what about the problem with the 255 divided by 19?

The student who had come up with a solution had to leave early. So, another student explains the thinking. She did 3 × 8.5 feet and got the 255 and divided 255 by 19. The teacher pointed out that this thinking was not helpful and crossed it out for right now, and she moved on to the solution 102 divided by 3. Students were given an opportunity to discuss this solution to make sense of it in small groups.

STUDENT: 12 × 8

TEACHER: Why 12 × 8?

STUDENT: Oh, because there are 8.5 feet. We did not want to do 8.5, so we did it to 8.

TEACHER: So, you left the decimal the hard part for later?

STUDENT: Yeah

TEACHER: Does everybody follow that thinking so far. They are just taking the 8 feet. Why by 12. The teacher writes 8 × 12 on the board?

STUDENT: Because there are 12 inches per one foot.

TEACHER: So, there are 12 inches for one foot? Penelope so why did she say that?

STUDENT: If there are 12 inches in 1 foot.

TEACHER: So, you have 8 feet.

STUDENTS: Wait, so you just add them up!

TEACHER: I heard you when you said 12 came from inches. Some of you went ahh! So why would that be important? 12 × 8 is what?

STUDENTS: 96

The teacher points out that we are not at 102.

STUDENT: And then we added 6.

TEACHER: Why?

STUDENT: Because you added the 6.

Teacher: Why don't you just add 0.5?

Students discuss in groups that 0.5 is 6 inches because it is half a foot. The class reaches the same conclusion. The class realizes that half of a foot is 6 inches. They figured out that 96 + 6 makes up 102, and it represents the distance of the whole fence and the 3 represents the 3-inch gap.

TEACHER: What happened to our units. We started here, and we had inches. (pointing to 8.5 divided by 3 inches. The class notices that they are dealing with different units that include inches and feet, inches and pickets and inches and inches.

TEACHER: Do the units matter?

STUDENTS: Yes!

TEACHER: We have to convert in the same units.

The teacher asks students their next step since they have figured out different ways to think about the problem. The teacher decides to further scaffold student thinking by giving them a simpler problem to think about.

• *Scaffolding student thinking by working a simpler problem*

The teacher provides students with a simpler problem with smaller numbers to help them think through the problem. She uses her figures to show a fence. She explains that she is going to use her thumb and pinkie to represent the posts, "Then with my fingers, I have three posts."

Teacher draws and shares her thinking using gestures.

TEACHER: So, how many spaces are there?

STUDENTS: Four.

TEACHER: Alright, I am dealing with four spaces.

Teacher tells the student that the total distance is 4 feet. She asks the students what tool she is using, and students respond that she is using a bar diagram.

TEACHER: I have four spaces, and from here, I want to know how many spaces I need to evenly divide my figures. She points out that each picket is 3 inches. Then they proceed to use the strategies on the board to convert the feet to inches. "12 × 4 = ?"The class figures out that they are working with 48 inches. The teacher says, "If I divide 48 by 3 that is not going to help me because that gets me to 12. So, I need to balance my total space of 48 how many spaces are already taken.

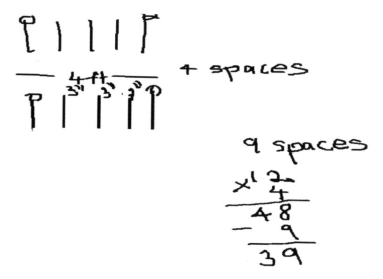

A student points out that it is 9 inches. So, the class figures out that the 9 inches are already taken. Students point out that you must subtract the 9 from the 48, which is the total distance. The teacher writes their explanation on the board as illustrated above.

STUDENTS: Ah!!!! Oh!!!

TEACHER: What do we get?

STUDENTS: 39

The class realizes that there are 39 inches left, and they have to divide it evenly by 4. The students have recess, and the teacher walks around and reflects on the class thinking.

• *The teacher reflects on student thinking*

Mrs. Sanchez notices that two groups have got it and another group has figured out the distance, and they need to divide it. She was unsure about one group's thinking, so she decides to have them start by explaining how they thought about it. She reads what they have written on the paper and reflects on how they are thinking. She notices that two groups have kept all their units in feet and that threw off their answer. She reflects that this makes it more difficult to get the answer.

• *Figuring out the answer to the original problem*

Students come back in from recess, and they worked on the original problem and discussed their solutions. Two students shared their thinking on how they got their answer to the original problem. One student explains that you have to divide the 45 by the 20 spaces and you get 2.25 as the answer. The teacher shifts the discussion from the focus of the original problem to figuring out how to divide decimals using long division and an area model because this had been the focus of the content covered in class for a couple of days. Also, they talked about representing the answer either as a fraction or as a decimal and the connections between the two.

The teacher was interested in assessing students' strategies for dividing numbers that result in a division answer. She has students write their solutions on the white board. This allowed her to assess student strategies of the division with decimals. The teacher makes explicit the big ideas of solving problems involving division with decimals and its relationship to representing a decimal as a fraction. The rich problem was an opportunity for students to engage in problem-solving.

This lesson illustrates a class working on a challenging, rich problem and figuring out answers by using the mathematics of decimals and division. Students had been learning about dividing decimals in their class unit, this problem represents an application problem. Neither every lesson nor discussion looks the same. The purpose must drive the discussion and the amount of time and scaffolding needed based on student thinking.

- *Scaffolding student thinking*

There were several strategies that Mrs. Sanchez used to scaffold student thinking. This was a complex problem to solve that involved more than simply applying a procedure. However, the tasks were built on students' prior knowledge, and Mrs. Sanchez said in her interview that she purposefully selected this task because it reviewed and applied dividing decimals and set the stage to learn about fractions on a number line.

Watch Teacher Interview: How Mrs. Sanchez planned a lesson and set up her classroom

Scaffolding is an essential part of supporting student learning.

- The problem was chosen because it was built on prior knowledge.
- She created the classroom environment for discussion to take place.

Watch the video on teacher interview on Writing and Math.

After the whole class discussion, Mrs. Sanchez has students journal their thinking. She explains that the goal is to have them reflect on the math and record their thinking. She also felt it was important that they should be able to refer to their discussion and teamwork. So, she viewed that it was a gradual release of thinking from small group, to whole group, to individual thinking.

Mrs. Sanchez looks for their mathematical reasoning such as the use of math vocabulary, sequencing how they got their answer, and are they able to explain that through words. She was also interested in learning about the individual strategies they used.

CHAPTER SUMMARY

The third level of planning involves making decisions on what to talk about during the lesson. This part involves responding to student thinking and mathematical goals. The teacher needs to pose a problem and formatively assess student reasoning and make a decision about what to address in discussion to move thinking forward and scaffold student reasoning so that they could successfully solve the problem as well as identify mathematical concepts and procedures.

STUDY GUIDE

STRATEGIES FOR THE CLASSROOM

Examining Student Work to Build the Whole Class Discussion

- As students are engaged in solving problems, walk around the room and observe students' reasoning processes.
- Record or make mental notes of types of strategies that are emerging (typically there will be four or five different ways the class is thinking). Consider which strategies are more effective.
- Pose questions to help students clarify thinking or provide helpful hints.
- Note misconceptions or errors that should be addressed in the discussion.
- Think about what background knowledge is revealed in student solutions (so that you can build discussion on what they already know).
- Think about the "big mathematical idea" you want students to get by of solving the problem.
- Identify a problem or issue to discuss that will challenge students' current thinking and build on what students are currently doing. (*Note:* Don't try to address every issue that comes up. Prioritize the issues for discussions. Pick one or two important issues to explore in depth.)
- Think about sequencing the discussion. What order should the solutions be presented?

The purpose of informally assessing student work and reasoning is to make decisions on how to support and extend student understanding and thinking.

Therefore, spending time looking only for right or wrong answers is not helpful. Checking who has the right and wrong answers will not give you enough information to know what students understand or do not understand. Furthermore, it is inefficient to individually tutor each child "the steps" to solve the problem. When students struggle to solve a problem, they are engaging in sense-making that supports learning.

Self-Reflection Questions

1. What is the value of the teacher walking around and observing student work? What should the teacher pay attention to when examining student work?
2. What is the difference between only looking at student answers to make sure that they are correct and understanding the process of student thinking about the solution?
3. What would you talk about in the whole class discussion? Why?

REFLECTING ON PRACTICE

Planning the Discussion

Curriculum/Pacing Guide

Date:_____ Lesson: _____
Use this worksheet during the discussion to informally assess students' thinking, errors, misconceptions, and representations to identify an issue to discuss.

Table 5.1 Decision-Making Process for Choosing Issue to Discuss

Math Concept/Skills	Types of Student Strategies/Errors and Misconceptions
Notes	Sequencing the discussion (solution types)
Goals for discussion	The problem to pose to get discussion started

CHAPTER VIDEO CASE REFLECTION QUESTIONS

Watch video 5.1: Fifth-Grade Problem-Solving Lesson (Division/Decimals)
Duration: 30 Minutes

1. Why did Mrs. Sanchez choose a rich problem lesson and how did it align with her instructional goals?

2. How did students make sense of the problem?

3. What was the role of the whole class discussion?

4. What kind of scaffolding took place in the lesson?

5. What was the role of assessment in driving the lesson?

6. What kind of learning took place?

Watch video 5.2: Teacher Interview: Writing and Math in Fifth-Grade Lesson
https://textbooks.rowman.com/lamberg

1. How did Mrs. Sanchez use writing in her math lesson?

2. What were Mrs. Sanchez's goals for integrating witting?

3. How did she assess writing? Why?

REFLECTING ON YOUR PRACTICE

1. Think about your lesson and the purpose of your lesson? (Practice concept, introduce a new concept, and engage in deep problem-solving. Clear up misconceptions and errors.)

2. How are you going to structure time?

3. What is the role of the lesson plan and discussion?

4. What are you going to assess? Why?

5. How are you going to use that information in your teaching?

6. How are you going to scaffold student thinking?

Chapter 6

The Discussion: Three Levels of Sense-Making

Teacher questioning has been identified as a critical part of teachers' work. The act of asking a good question that is cognitively demanding, requires considerable pedagogical content knowledge, and necessitates that teachers know their learners well (Boaler & Brodie, 2004).

Teachers can effectively use questions during the whole class discussion to help students clarify their thinking and to challenge them to think more deeply about the ideas presented. Students' understanding and conceptions are either refined or changed as they reflect on questions that are posed by the teacher. These questions make a bridge between students' current understanding and mathematical goals. During a conversation, students typically accept and assimilate each other's ideas, disagree, change their minds, or reinvent new ideas (Martino & Maher, 1999). The next step is learning how to use teacher's questioning to facilitate mathematical connections during the whole class discussion.

POSING A QUESTION TO START THE WHOLE CLASS DISCUSSION

Pose a question to start a discussion; for example, a discussion with young children might begin by asking them if the number sentence $6 + 9 = 7 - 2 + 10$ is true. To answer this question, students will likely use multiple strategies such as $6 + 9 = 5 + 10 = 15$ or $7 - 2 = 5 + 10 = 15$. Some students might conclude that the answer should be 15 because they believe that the answer comes after the equal sign.

This problem can generate a meaningful discussion only if it has the appropriate level of challenge based on students' prior knowledge and background.

Students should experience some level of difficulty, and the problem should potentially result in a range of answers or models. If the problem is too easy, students will know the answer, and there will be nothing to talk about. Similarly, choosing a problem that is too difficult for students is also not very useful either. Students need to have some entry point to tackle the problem. The mathematical goals for students and their current understandings should guide the direction of the conversation.

Using Questions to Identify Discussion Topics

Guided questions during the discussion can lead students to identify problems and issues to explore and discuss. For example, consider the following problem—if six children share eight pies equally, how much pie will each child get?—the teacher might help students figure out how to partition a circle correctly by asking, "How do you decide how many equal parts you need to cut each pizza into?" This question would require students to think about the concept of partitioning, equal shares, and fair sharing situations. Students will have to discover that equal sharing situations require cutting the whole into equal amounts; the whole unit has to be cut into shares that represent multiples of the divisors. In this situation, it is the students, not the teacher, who are defining the problem. As students engage in solving problem individually and in small groups, more questions or issues may come up.

Problem-posing can lead to critical thinking and a deeper understanding of mathematical ideas (Brown & Walter, 2005). Questions such as "What is the problem asking?" can be explored. Many times, students are unable to solve a problem because they do not understand what the problem is asking them in the first place—asking "what if" questions involves modifying a problem, which requires students to reconceptualize the problem and use a different approach to problem-solve. For example, a student or teacher could ask what would happen if numbers in a problem were changed. For example, what if 10 children, instead of 6, shared 8 pies equally? What would happen to each child's share?

By asking "what if" questions, the students must think about the role of the divisor and the dividend in the problem. This can lead to the exploration of the idea that the larger the denominator, the smaller the resulting answer. In other words, each child would get less pie because more people are sharing the pies.

After a question has been posed, students need time to work with partners or small groups to think about the problem. The teacher should observe students' reasoning and then choose the order in which students will present their solutions. Students with lower-level strategies using more concrete approaches can share first. Students with more abstract and sophisticated strategies can share later. The next section describes the different levels of sense-making and the types of questions that get at these layers of sense-making see figure 6.1.

THE THREE LEVELS OF SENSE-MAKING IN DISCUSSION

Teacher questioning can be used to unpack meaning throughout the three levels of a whole class discussion. Figure 6.1 illustrates the layers of sense-making in a conversation that will lead to new mathematical insights. The first phase involves communicating clearly so that everyone can understand each other's perspective.

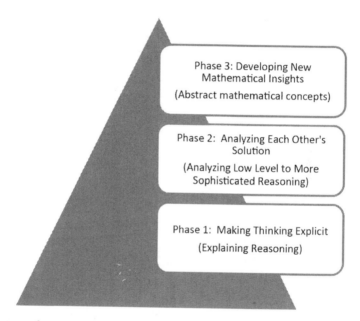

Phase 3: Developing New Mathematical Insights

(Abstract mathematical concepts)

Phase 2: Analyzing Each Other's Solution

(Analyzing Low Level to More Sophisticated Reasoning)

Phase 1: Making Thinking Explicit

(Explaining Reasoning)

Figure 6.1. Three Levels of Sense Making

The second phase involves comparing and analyzing each other's point of view. This is different than just sharing information. A higher level of critical thinking takes place when students evaluate, compare, and contrast each other's strategies and make connections between each other's point of view.

The third phase of conversation involves taking the conversation to a much deeper level that leads to mathematical generalizations, or the "big mathematical ideas" students arrived at. Formal mathematics such as formulas and definitions or a summary of a "big mathematical idea" can be introduced at this point. This is the kind of knowledge that can transfer to other problem situations.

Phase 1: Making Thinking Explicit. Students' explanations make meaningful contributions to the discussion only if the whole class can understand the ideas being presented. An explanation given by a student is useful only when the other students can follow it. Otherwise, students can tune out of the conversation or become confused. The teacher can ask questions to scaffold the student's explanation, monitor whether the students understand the explanation and are paying attention, and have students restate the explanation in their own words. Students can use drawings and models to enhance their explanations. Pointing to part of the model or drawing helps the class see what a student is referring to.

The sequence of presentation of the student explanations should be carefully considered. It is much easier to follow student explanations if the ideas are presented from the more simplistic level to the more sophisticated. This allows students to gain knowledge that will help them understand more complex ideas. All students do not need to present explanations; it is sufficient to present a few different strategies. Sample questions, which can be used to help students explain and clarify their thinking, are provided at the end of the chapter.

CASE STUDY: CLARIFYING AN EXPLANATION

Scenario: The teacher presented this problem to her fifth-grade students: "If five children equally shared six packs of gum that had five pieces in each pack, how much would each child get?" Students could think about the unit in the problem as "packs of gum," "pieces of gum," or simultaneously as "packs and pieces."

The Discussion: Sam presented his solution (See Figure 6.2). The teacher posed questions to the class to make sure they understood what Sam was thinking.

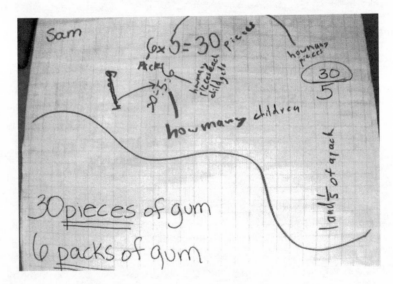

Figure 6.2.   Sam's Strategy

SAM: How many pieces are in a pack? It becomes to be 30 pieces of gum. Five sticks represent "how many children." Thirty divided by five equals six, and the six equals "how many pieces of gum each child gets." (See Figure 6.2 Sam's Strategy)

TEACHER: Anyone wants to try and explain what he was thinking? Sam did a good job, but sometimes it helps to have another student walk through it. Corey?

COREY: I think what Sam was doing was, he was trying to figure out the problem by just using number sentences. Like he is drawing here, it is a really short number sentence. I put these two together to make a true number sentence.

TEACHER: Can you tell me how Sam was thinking about math? You just explained his method. Walk us through what exactly Sam was doing here.

COREY: Well, what I think he was doing was that he was writing the number sentences.

TEACHER: Can you explain what each of those pieces represents in the number sentence? I notice that the six in the number sentence is not labeled. What do you think the six represents?

COREY: I would think that the six represents pieces or something.

KAREN: It represents the six packs.

TEACHER: It represents the pack? Would you add that word there?

Analysis: Sam explained; however, because the teacher did not feel that the students understood his explanation, she asked another student to explain what Sam thought so that students would analyze his solution. Corey pointed out that Sam did not draw a picture as the other students had; instead, he used number sentences to represent his work. To make students dig deeper into Sam's mathematical thinking, the teacher redirected the conversation and asked more specific questions. She asked what the numbers in Sam's number sentence represented about the problem. She wanted students to notice that Sam was thinking about the unit in terms of packs and pieces: 6×5 represented 6 packs of gum times 5 pieces in each pack, for a total of 30 pieces. The teacher wanted students to understand the larger mathematical goal that visualizing the unit can influence how you solve the problem. Furthermore, there are many ways to visualize the unit.

Phase 2: Analyzing Each Other's Solutions to Make Connections. When students are expected to analyze each other's solutions, they need to think about the student's explanation, and decide if the answer makes sense and connects to other ideas presented in the discussion. The students must be actively listening to benefit from the discussion. (Chapter 3 described what active listening looks like.) When students listen and actively participate, they will eventually learn that listening and thinking about their explanations support their learning (Martino & Maher, 1999). In other words, as they listen they should think about how what another student is saying relates to their thinking.

Therefore, students have to engage in critical thinking instead of passively listening to student explanations. For example, to solve a fair sharing problem, one student might come up with a solution of 1/2 and another with 2/4. Students can deepen their understanding of mathematics by examining how these solutions are similar and different. For example, a student can prove that 2/4 and 1/2 are the same amount. On the other hand, students can explore that even though they are equivalent, the whole unit is partitioned differently. Also, students are also learning that the problem can be solved in multiple ways, which leads to flexibility in thinking and number sense.

Comparing solutions also enables students to see connections between simpler and more sophisticated answers. In addition, students also need to work toward developing more efficient strategies for solving problems (Cobb, Yackel, & McClain, 2000). For example, there are many ways to solve the problem $20 \div 5$. The following solutions are presented from simple to more sophisticated and represent a continuum from least to most efficient:

1. Distribute 20 blocks into 5 piles and count how many pieces are in a pile
2. Draw 20 circles and circle groups of 5
3. Use tally marks grouped in 5s
4. Add $5 + 5 + 5 + 5$
5. Multiply 5×4

Eventually, students should work toward using more efficient strategies to accurately solve problems; however, understanding how the inefficient strategies contribute to the more efficient strategies develops students' number sense. For example, if students don't have an image that 5×4 is 5 groups of 4, then they don't have a deep understanding of multiplication as a concept. Just memorizing $5 \times 4 = 20$ without understanding what it means represents a shallow understanding of mathematics. If students forget the memorized answer, they may be unable to figure out the answer or to use this knowledge as a tool to solve other problems.

The goal is to use the discussion to help students develop these layers of understanding to develop proficiency in mathematics. Figure 6.3 illustrates the continuum of understanding from inefficient to efficient strategies. The ultimate goal is for students to become proficient in solving mathematical problems using the most efficient strategies.

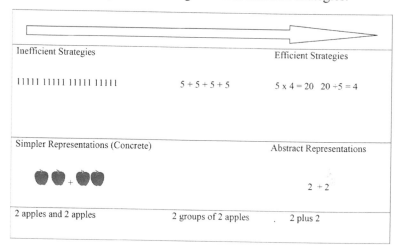

Figure 6.3 Continuum of Understanding the meaning of symbols and their mathematical meaning has been called "mathematizing" (Cobb, Yackel, & McClain, 2001). Students develop a more sophisticated understanding of mathematics through discussion using drawings and models to represent thinking. Because students don't naturally make these connections, the teacher can pose questions to help students see how strategies relate to each other. When students see connections between various strategies, they develop a more sophisticated understanding of mathematics in addition to number sense. Furthermore, students who have varied ability levels in solving the problem can participate in the conversation.

Phase 3: Developing New Mathematical Insights by Making Generalizations. The purpose of the discussion is to help students gain new mathematical insights (big ideas) that can transfer to new problem-solving situations. After students have explored different strategies to solve a problem, they need to clearly understand the underlying mathematical concepts they learned. Therefore, students must come up with a rule or a summary of key mathematical ideas they learn from the discussion. The group needs a shared understanding of what these ideas mean.

Case study: Writing a number sentence to represent a fair sharing problem

Scenario: The students solved two problems: (1) If six children share eight pies equally, how much pie will each get? (2) If eight children share six pies equally, how much pie will each child get? The teacher observed that many students were confused about how to write the number sentence and mixed up the divisor and the dividend. Also, they did not think about how the division resulted in a fractional answer as an algebraic relation between the divisor and dividend.

The Lesson: The teacher writes the essential information about these two problems on two chart papers and displays them next to each other to confront students about the meaning of the divisor and the dividend, its division relationship, and the size of the resulting answer (see Figure 6.4).

The teacher starts the conversation by asking, "Which quotient will be less than one?" Students must think about the dividend and divisor as a number sentence. This requires students to engage in algebraic thinking.

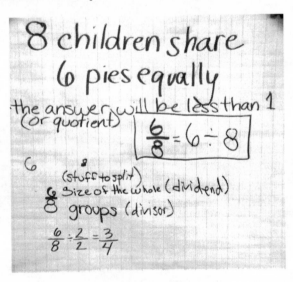

Figure 6.4. Exploring meaning of divisor and dividend

NATALIE: That one! (She points to the chart paper with "six children share eight pies equally." See Figure 6.4)

TEACHER: You think it is going to be this one? Why, Natalie?

NATALIE: There are going to be six pies and eight children. There will not be enough for them to get one whole.

The teacher writes, "The answer will be less than one or quotient."

Analysis: The teacher scaffolds the student's explanation by writing the key information on the chart paper to clarify what Natalie means and also makes her thinking explicit so that other students can think about her explanation. This written record of her thinking can be referred to in the subsequent discussions. By writing the word *quotient*, the teacher is introducing math vocabulary. The teacher asks the class to raise their hands if they agree with Natalie's answer. As a result, the teacher can quickly assess student thinking.

> *TEACHER:* Look at this problem (See Figure 6.5)—six children share eight pies equally. Is the answer going to be more or less than one?

> *SALINA:* Greater than one, because each child will receive more than one pie.

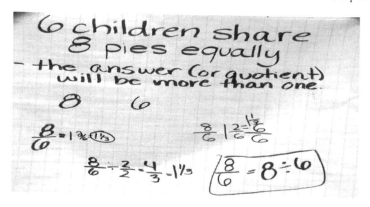

Figure 6.5.   Predicting size of Quotient

> *TEACHER:* Okay. The answer or quotient will be more than one. Which number represents the things we are going to split up? Which number is called the dividend?

> *STUDENT:* 8.

> *TEACHER:* Okay, I'll write 8 on the chart. Let's look again at the problem. There are eight pies divided by six children equally. Can someone come up and write what they think is the "stuff to split"? We are going to call that the "size of the whole." Which of the two numbers is it—the eight or six? Which is going to represent the numbers that we are going to share?

Analysis: The teacher is asking students to think about the problem context and identify the dividend. She refers to the dividend as the "size of the whole," or "stuff to split," wording which the students had used to describe the dividend. A student approaches the chart and writes the number 6 to represent the dividend. Then the teacher asks students to identify the divisor in the problem situation. She asks, "What number represents the groups that we are going to split this stuff into?" Another student writes the number 8. The teacher wants students to think about the meaning of numbers about the divisor and dividend. The teacher asks students to represent the division relationship as a fraction. Another student approaches the chart and writes 6/8.

> *TEACHER:* Thank you. What does that represent? What does 6/8 represent there?
>
> *STUDENT:* I think the 6/8 represents . . . the 6 represents how many pies are there, and the 8 represents how many children are there.

Analysis: The student is thinking about the division relationship between the divisor and dividend. The teacher asks students to think about what the 6/8 represents in relation to the problem context.

> *TEACHER:* Does anyone remember what I called it?
>
> *SALINA:* The size of the whole?
>
> *TEACHER:* What does the 8 represent?
>
> *STUDENT:* It could be the groups of the whole.
>
> *TEACHER:* Yes, that is when we divide the whole into the groups; we are going to split up. This (pointing) represents the whole we are going to split up. We call this the dividend and this the divisor (writes next to the fraction).
>
> *TEACHER:* So, I want to go back to the 6/8 again. How can we say this? So, what does the line represent? (points to the fraction bar)
>
> *STUDENT:* Division.
>
> *TEACHER:* How will we say this, if we say it as a division problem?
>
> *STUDENT:* 6 divided by 8.

Analysis: The teacher wants students to see the connection between the fraction representation of the problem and division by focusing on the meaning of the fraction. She inserts the math vocabulary *divisor* and *dividend* into the discussion.

Next, the teacher writes $6/8 = 6 \div 8$. Then she writes $8/6 = 8 \div 6$. A student makes the connection that the fractions represent division.

Teacher: When you look at these two problems, what do you notice comes first in the division problem? Is it the size of the whole? Or is it the groups?

Analysis: This question forces students to compare problem situations. The teacher explains that in a number sentence, the "stuff to split"

(8) appears first and the number of groups (6) appears after the division sign. In a fraction, the size of the whole goes above the fraction bar and appears as the numerator. The number below the fraction line is called the denominator and represents the number of groups.

Conclusion: The lesson ends with the teacher and students creating a generalization. In this whole class discussion, the teacher used questions to get students to think about the meaning of the divisor and dividend by writing a number sentence. She scripted (wrote student responses on the chart (See Figure 6.6)) while the students explained their answers. The class generated a rule during the whole class discussion that can be tested and applied for other problems involving equal sharing situations.

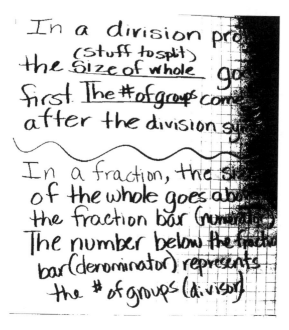

Figure 6.6. Making Big Mathematical Ideas Explicit

Note that the case study exemplifies why a discussion should not begin with a generalization. If a discussion begins with a rule, students may end up memorizing the rule without understanding what it means. When students solve a problem during a discussion, they develop an understanding of the rule, which they can apply in other contexts. This also means that students are more likely to remember the rule.

CHAPTER SUMMARY

The questions the teacher asks during a discussion depend on the purpose and the situation. It is important to select the right problem to start the discussion. Problems should not be too difficult or too simplistic; they must also have the potential for mathematical issues to emerge that fit with the mathematical goals and student understanding. Once a problem has been posed to get the discussion started, the discussion should progress through the three levels of sense-making discussion presented in this chapter.

The first level involves making thinking explicit. Selected students share their reasoning while ensuring everyone in the class understands the explanation. The second level requires critical analysis of student solutions to make mathematical connections between different ways of solving problems. During this phase, students can address misconceptions and errors in thinking. The third level of understanding involves developing more abstract mathematical ideas and skills that can transfer to new situations. Carefully sequencing how students present solutions and discussions makes it easier for students to make mathematical connections because they can follow the arguments presented.

STUDY GUIDE

The purpose of the three levels of sense-making is to help students make sense of mathematical thinking and move thinking forward. Look at the "Strategies for your Classroom" and adapt the framework to your lesson. You don't need to ask all the questions. These are suggestions. The important part is to remember the purpose of what you are trying to accomplish at each level. Try printing these questions out (page 91), have it in a clipboard and practice using these levels of questioning to move thinking forward.

Videotape Lesson: Videotape a lesson and analyze the kinds of questioning and discussion that is taking place?

1. Look at the levels of sense-making and identify what levels are happening in the discussion.
2. Identify areas of strengths and weaknesses and practice using these levels.

Observe Classroom or Videotape of Discussion

• Analyze the kind of discussion that is taking place and the three levels of sense-making.
• What recommendations would you give the teacher based on the three levels of sense-making?

STRATEGIES FOR YOUR CLASSROOM

The sequence of a whole class discussion:

- Pose a question or problem.
- Discuss key vocabulary and clarify the general idea.
- Give time for students to work in groups to solve problem and record work in a math journal.
- Transition students to a whole group.
- Call for answers and record them on the board as students share thinking with others.
- Invite students to explain which answer they support and why.
- Call on students to ask questions or share their answers and solution on the board.
- Ask if students want to change their answers. Why?
- Arrive at a consensus for the answer. Make mathematical ideas explicit.
- Assign students a similar problem to solve on their own (optional).

Three Levels of Questions

See Figure 6.1.

Phase 1: Making Thinking Explicit

Questions to help students share and clarify their thinking:

- What are you thinking?
- How do you know that?
- Is there another way you can show it?
- Can you show us how you did that?
- How did you figure that out?
- Can you prove what you are thinking?
- What is the problem asking you to do?
- Is there another way to show how you solved the problem?
- Why did you think about it that way?
- Can you explain that part?

Questions to clarify if students understand the explanation:

- Does everyone understand _____'s solution?
- Who can explain what _____ is thinking?
- Which part are you having trouble following?

Chapter 6

Phase 2: Analyzing Solutions (from Low Level to More Sophisticated Reasoning)

Teacher questions to promote analysis and reflection:

- What do you see that is the same about these solutions?
- What do you see that is different about these solutions?
- How does this strategy relate to (the mathematical concept)?

Phase 3: Developing New Mathematical Insights

Teacher questions to promote mathematical insights

- What do these numbers mean?
- Can you come up with a rule or summarize the key idea?
- Will the rule work all the time?
- How will you use this rule to solve another problem?

Chapter 7

Reflect and Improve Teaching to Support Learning

Whole class discussions must be situated in the *process of teaching* to ensure that students make mathematical connections. Sequencing is critical for supporting student learning. The *process of teaching* involves thinking about physical space, classroom routines, lesson planning, and the discussion. All these components must work together to optimize students' opportunities to learn. This chapter focuses on strategies to improve your teaching so that they include effective whole class discussions to improve teaching. This framework has been tested and refined by hundreds of teachers. Here are some of the ways that the whole class discussion framework has been integrated. The goal is to use this book as a toolbox in a meaningful way to help you get results in student learning.

SCHOOL-LEVEL/GRADE-LEVEL/INDIVIDUAL BOOK STUDY

Get together as a school or in grade-level teams and fill out the *Levels of Implementation* rubric provided at the end of the chapter. Identify an area that you or your team would like to work on. Or an area that you would like to focus on individually. This could be done as an individual or as a team. Read the corresponding chapter related to each section of the framework and identify the strengths and weaknesses of your teaching. You can use this framework to keep track of the improvements that you are making.

Figure out what you would like to improve (See Figure 7.1). Identify some strategies and try them out in your classroom. Working together with other teachers makes it easier and more motivating. Working together with others allows you to have a support system. Teaching is a complex profession, so having a support system helps. Celebrate when you start seeing results, and focus on other aspects of the framework.

IMPROVING WHOLE CLASS DISCUSSIONS

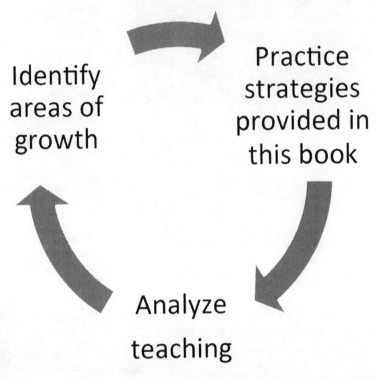

Figure 7.1. Improving Teaching Cycle

Making Classroom Teaching Visible to Improve Discussion

Improving techniques used to facilitate effective whole class discussions involves figuring out both strengths and the areas in need of growth (See Figure 7.1). This requires teachers to notice what they currently do and its impact on student understanding. A teacher's ability to notice things depends on what he or she is focusing on (Jacobs, Lamb, & Philipp, 2010). Not everyone "sees" the same things and makes the same interpretations. Therefore, having a lens to examine a lesson or a videotape is helpful. Rubrics, such as those provided at the end of this chapter, can help you pay attention to different aspects of your discussion.

Improving whole class discussions ultimately requires us to *change* what we do that is not working. Most of us have established many classroom routines that have become automatic. Therefore, the first step is to make our routines visible so that we can examine what is going on.

Videotape or Audiotape a Lesson. Videotaping or audiotaping a lesson is a powerful tool to self-evaluate teaching. This process allows you to step back and notice things. Think about what you want to focus on when looking at the videotape such as classroom routines and the kinds of conversations that are taking place. Identifying a focus area to look at in the videotape will help you notice more things.

Watch a videotape of a lesson with a friend(s). It is important to build trust and friendship to have conversations that are honest and helpful. Others might see and point out things in the video that you might have missed. The goal is to form a learning community.

Many teachers have found that transcribing a brief segment (5 to 10 minutes of the discussion) of the whole class discussion very helpful to make visible the actual conversation taking place. Specifically look at the nature of student interaction, teacher interaction, and questioning techniques.

Peer Observation. Ask a colleague to observe your teaching and give you feedback or observe a colleague's class to gain another perspective on how someone else approaches a discussion. Observation rubrics are provided at the end of this chapter. Rubrics can be adapted to focus on particular areas.

Lesson Study. In a lesson study, a group of teachers and an expert (such as a math coach) jointly plan a lesson and set lesson goals for the lesson. One teacher teaches the lesson while others observe and take notes without interfering. The lesson is revised based on the debriefing that takes place after the lesson (Fernandez 2002; Lewis, Perry, & Hurd, 2009). Next, a newly revised lesson is designed and taught. This approach is particularly valuable if you are working on a series of lessons over time. The advantage of this approach is that lessons can be developed and then refined over time based on the insight of multiple perspectives. The whole group should be meeting regularly.

Working with a Math Coach/Teacher Leader. A math coach has expert knowledge in teaching mathematics. Working with a math coach is a good way for teachers to reflect and change their practice of teaching (Race, Ho, & Bower, 2002). A math coach can challenge teachers to critically examine their techniques by asking questions and providing feedback. The math coach can observe discussions and design a plan to work on areas that can be refined. He or she may also have additional resources to help you.

TEACHER PROFESSIONAL DEVELOPMENT/IN-SERVICE COURSES

There are four aspects to the framework:

- Setting up the physical space
- Developing classroom routines
- Lesson planning
- Three levels of sense-making.

Here are some strategies you can use if you are a teacher educator, a math coach, or you do teacher professional development training. The best way to introduce the framework is to have teachers and pre-service teachers learn math through this approach and make the framework explicit and reflect on how it contributed to their math learning. For example, have teachers and pre-service teachers solve a complex math problem and think about how the small-group discussion contributed to student learning. When looking at research and studying math concepts, connect it to the first level of planning where you are creating concept maps to explore interconnections of mathematics. Embed this framework in content-based professional development.

Working with students and classroom experiences are powerful. Try these strategies in the classroom if you are a teacher, or in a practicum setting if you are a pre-service teacher. Realize that these strategies take about a year to implement even if you are an experienced teacher. The best part is you will see results in student learning! This will motivate you to keep refining your teaching. As teachers, we are all lifelong learners!

STRATEGIES FOR IMPLEMENTING THE FRAMEWORK

- Experience math learning as a learner through a problem-solving approach and discussion as outlined by the framework. Reflect on how this approach contributed to their own learning.
- Connect framework to Learning Math Content (Content Knowledge, Pedagogical Content Knowledge)
- Connect Framework to Lesson Planning (Pedagogy)
- Connect Framework to Children's Mathematical Thinking (Professional Noticing, Formative Assessment)—Connect to Classrooms
- Connect Framework to Discussions—(Common Core Standards for Mathematical Practice, CCSSM, 2010)

Setting Up the Physical Space

• Read chapter 2 and reflect on how to organize physical space. Use checklist and evaluate classroom arrangement to ensure that there is space for the whole group to meet facing a focal point, In addition, make sure there is space for students to be able to walk to the board and access materials during small-group discussions; the teacher needs to be able to walk around to listen and monitor small-group discussions.

Pre-Service Teacher: Visit a math class and look at the checklist and think about how the physical space contributes to learning.

• Create a design of your ideal classroom.

Developing Classroom Routines

• Read chapter 3. Think about how classroom routines contribute to student learning. Examine the classroom videos provided in this book, and others identify classroom routines and the impact on student learning. Think about how to establish routines for discussion.
• Videotape a lesson, and examine your classroom routines' strengths and weaknesses. If you can observe each other's classrooms and provide feedback, you could also videotape a lesson and debrief at a grade-level group if you are comfortable sharing.
• Identifies strengths and weaknesses and try implementing strategies listed in chapter 3.

Note: It takes time to establish these routines. This is not difficult, but you need to consistently apply routines for discussion and listening. Keep instructions simple. This makes it easier to implement.
Pre-Service Teacher: Observe a math class or watch videos and write about classroom routines and how they contribute to student learning.

Lesson Planning

First Level of Planning: Teachers can study research on the content domains of the state standards and create concept maps and explore the progression of topics across the grade levels.

Look at the Table of Contents of the math curriculum and examine how the topics are laid out for the school year. The goal is to pay attention to sequencing to understand how the topics build on each other. This will help with pacing your lessons more efficiently.

Note: The goal of the first level of planning is to have a clear idea of what mathematics content your students need to learn and how it is laid out during the school year so that you can adjust your teaching to help students learn. Also, you and your students would be able to see interconnections between the topics and how they build on each other.

For example, understanding place value is important to learn how to add. Therefore, spending time on place value will help students learn how to add much faster instead of struggling with gaps in their learning. (See video case study at the end of this chapter.) The top two bullets should be completed before the start of the school year. The reality is that once the school year starts, it is hard to find time to do this level of deep thinking.

Weekly Lesson Plan: Create a unit plan using the tools provided in chapter 4. The goal is to plan for the week. You are not completing a detailed lesson plan but looking at how the lessons build on each other and thinking about how students will respond based on your assessment of your students. You are also laying out a learning trajectory (learning path) that you anticipate that your students might follow. This way, you know where you are headed with each lesson.

Second Level of Planning: Think about how to use your math time to optimize learning. Look at chapter 5 to think about how to use your instruction time constructively. This is planning the daily lesson. This is what you do during your prep time or after school. Planning each lesson requires careful thought because you need to build on formative and summative assessment data.

Your goal is to help students make connections and learn new information by building on their prior knowledge. Therefore, paying close attention to student learning and adapting your lessons, which includes tasks and pacing activities, will help you make more targeted decisions to help your students learn.

Formative assessment is an important part of good teaching. Anticipating what students might do and knowing what to notice and assess will help you decide on your next instructional move. During and after your lessons, figure out ways to keep track of class and individual thinking. Checklists provided in chapter 5 are a powerful way to keep track of individual and class thinking. These checklists should correspond to your concept maps. Mathematics and student thinking should drive your teaching.

Third Level of Planning: This level involves adapting the lesson to meet the needs of students while teaching. Plan the next instructional moves based on a formative assessment of student thinking during teaching, while keeping in mind the big mathematical idea embedded in instruction. Specifically, think about the role of discussion, individual thinking, partner/small-group work, and how to move thinking forward.

Three Levels of sense-making. During whole class discussion Reach in chapter 5 and practice strategies. A powerful way is to videotape and reflect on the three levels of sense-making. Many teachers tend to do the level one, and it requires some effort when you move toward having level two and three in your discussions. These are three easy strategies to remember.

1. making thinking explicit
2. analyzing each other's' solutions
3. making big ideas explicit

CHAPTER SUMMARY

Facilitating effective whole class discussions can make your teaching more effective and efficient. You can address the needs of diverse learners by giving them opportunities to communicate and analyze multiple representations. Therefore, investing the time to hold whole class discussions is well worth the effort. You can introduce new information that builds on student thinking and challenges students to think more deeply about the concepts explored.

The NCTM and the Common Core standards both point out the importance of communication in supporting students to learn math. A whole class discussion is only a part of the conversations that should take place within a math lesson. It does not replace the small group, partner talk, or conversations with individual students. Instead, it builds, synthesizes, and extends these conversations. Furthermore, the whole class discussion is the place where the class as a whole can develop a shared understanding of the mathematical issue.

Once you have identified areas that you would like to work on, select one or two skills at a time to work on. Understand how these skills fit with the larger picture of supporting mathematical learning through whole class discussions. The more your practice these skills, the easier it will become. The most important thing to remember is to keep reflecting on what you are doing. Is it working? Why or why not?

STUDY GUIDE

Whole Class Mathematics Discussions: Improving In-Depth Mathematical Thinking and Learning Framework

Please indicate the level of implementation (Rate 0–4)

0—Not implemented

1—Starting to implement—Still figuring out how to implement this part of the framework

2—Implemented—Becoming more comfortable using these strategies in teaching, using some of the time

3—Implemented—Implemented strategies, using most of the time

4—Fully Implemented—Consistently using these strategies as a regular part of my teaching

Not implemented ———————————————→ Fully Implemented

	0	1	2	3	4
Setting up the Classroom					
Setting up Physical Space					
Cultivating Classroom Environment/Routines					
Routines for Preparing for Discussion					
Routines for Communicating					
Routines for Listening/Reflecting					
Lesson Planning					
First level Planning (Long term & Short Term Goals) Concepts (big ideas) Unit Plan (Sequencing/learning trajectory)					
Second Level of Planning 5 E-Lesson Plan- (Anticipating Student Reasoning/Misconceptions Errors, The format for using a problem-solving approach to teaching and structuring time)					
Third Level of Planning (Adapting discussion to support student understanding/needs) Making decisions on what to talk about based on student reasoning during lessons					

Teacher Questioning/ Supporting Mathematical Connections					
Three Levels of Sense-Making					
Phase 1: Making Thinking explicit					
Phase II: Analyzing Each other's solutions					
Phase III: Developing New Mathematical Insights					

Comments:

CASE STUDY

Video Case: Two-Digit Addition with Regrouping

CLASS: Grade 2

TEACHER: Ms. Akbar

Ms. Akbar's goal is to introduce her second-grade students to the partial sums method. Her plan is to have students discover this method of addition on their own. Students are given base-10 blocks to use as they individually work to solve an addition problem involving two digits. Ms. Akbar realized as she was teaching the lesson that her students lacked the background knowledge on place value that she expected them to have from the prior grade. She reflected on her next instructional moves to support students develop place value.
Watch video clip 7.1: Two-Digit Addition with Regrouping, Class 2 (00:16:34)
https://textbooks.rowman.com/lamberg
Watch video clip 7.2: Second-Grade Teacher Interview: Class 2. (00:05:07)
https://textbooks.rowman.com/lamberg

Reflecting on Video 6.1: Second-Grade Lesson: Two-Digit Addition

As you watch students explain their reasoning, consider the following questions:

1. What does the student understand mathematically?
2. What is the student confused about?
3. What would be a potential teaching point?
4. What questions might you pose to get students to clarify their misconceptions or confusions?
5. What learning took place?
6. How did the teacher use questioning to facilitate connections?
7. How did the teacher address misconceptions and errors?
8. How would the students have responded if the teacher started the discussion by showing students "step by step" on how to use the manipulatives to model the problem?
9. Why is it important to let students figure things out for themselves? When should a teacher intervene?
10. If you were the teacher, how would you have responded?

What are her next steps?

Reflecting on Video 6.1: Second-Grade Lesson: Two-Digit Addition

1. How did the teacher use her informal assessment of student reasoning to change her questioning?
2. How did the teacher support students to make connections between the problem, manipulatives, and written symbols?
3. What insights did you gain from listening to the teacher interview?
4. What would you do if the discussion took a different direction than expected? How would you prepare for such a situation?
5. What would you do next if you were the teacher?

Ms. Akbar begins the lesson by asking students to solve the problem $27 + 48$. She chose this particular problem because it involves regrouping. (She had not officially introduced regrouping yet.) In previous lessons, the students had done two-digit addition without regrouping. Students work at their desks to solve the problem and then share their solutions during the whole group discussion.

Jacob's Explanation

Jacob uses his 100 chart to figure out the answer. He adds the 20 + 40 to get 60. Then he adds 8 to make 68. He counted 7 more up from 68 to get 75.

Tristen's Explanation

Tristen presents what he wrote in his journal. He concludes that the answer is 408. His solution is illustrated in figure 7.3.

2	0
2	9
4	9

409

Figure 7.3. Tristen's Solution

Tristen explains that he built the number 20 by using two rods representing 10 units. Next, he added 9 to get the 29 and counted 27 individual blocks. (He had incorrectly written 29 instead of 27.) At this point, he pauses, because he is unsure about how to proceed.

Analysis: It appears that Tristen added 20 and 20 to get 49 and then concluded that he needed to add the zero in there, arriving at getting 409. When asked why he got 409, he explains that he was using the "partial sums method." This is an example of a student applying a rule without understanding the meaning behind it. Tristen has some knowledge of addition, but his answer does not makes sense.

At this point, Ms. Akbar has to decide on how to proceed. She has to consider what Tristen did understand, as well as what he did not. She must also think about how other students can benefit from the discussion to proceed as well. She instructs Tristen to work through the problem again and poses questions to the class to keep them involved and help them define their thought processes.

Student 3's Explanation

Ms. Akbar asks another student to help Tristen figure out the answer in an easier way. She points out that Tristen has counted out 27 individual blocks, thus validating what he did correctly. She also makes explicit how the 27 unit blocks related to the problem context.

> *TEACHER:* How can we help Tristen add 48 in there? He's got 27 already. How can he add 48 to that?
>
> *STUDENT 3:* With the 10s and the 1s.
>
> *TEACHER:* Ooh, the 10s and 1s. How can you add them?
>
> *STUDENT 3:* You can do 4 tens . . . and then 8 cubes and add 27 to it.

Analysis: As the student explains, Ms. Akbar models the explanation with blocks so that the rest of the class can visualize the explanation. She asks Tristen to explain further how to physically add the 27 individual blocks and the 4 rods and the 8 blocks. After he works with the blocks, she asks Tristen to return to his desk to figure out the answer.

Thea's Explanation

Thea correctly solves the problem, using informal methods to represent the 10s and the units. She explains that she added 2 + 4 to get 6 and then added 7 + 8 to get 15.

> *TEACHER:* How does 7 +8 equal to 75?
>
> *STUDENT:* I had 60, and I added 15.
>
> *TEACHER:* What do you mean 60? You have a 2 and 4 (pointing to student writing).

Thea explains that the 2 + 4 makes up 60. Then she counted up and thought about the 7 + 8 as 7 + 3 + 5. She concludes that the answer is 75. Ms. Akbar asks students to put their thumbs up if they agree with the answer. Some students put their thumbs up while others did not. Ms. Akbar asks if anyone else added the 10s first. Six students raise their hands. Cameron comes up and provides the same explanation as Thea. **Analysis:** Ms. Akbar discovered that students had some background knowledge and strategies to add two-digit numbers with regrouping. One of her goals was to get students to develop more efficient ways to solve the problems besides individually counting all the blocks.

(See video clip 6.2.) She wants to help them understand the concept of trading 10 individual blocks for one rod representing a unit of 10.

She asks the class to build a model using base-10 rods to explain what the numbers in the problem represent. In doing so, she is asking students to connect their written number symbols with the place value models. Students look at 6 rods, which represent 60, and 15 blocks.

> *TEACHER:* How that can equal 75?
>
> *STUDENT:* The 15 has a 10 in it. Then you just add the 10 and it gets 70, and you have 5 ones left over.

The student further explains that you can trade 10 individual blocks for one rod, and then add it to the 60 and get 70. Then you add the 5 plus 70 and get 75.

> *TEACHER:* Who can show me that? Alandro, come on up and show me that.
>
> *ALANDRO:* You take 10 of the blocks, and trade them for a long one, and then you have to use the rest of the 5s, and that will be 75.

Ms. Akbar clarifies what the student said and demonstrated how 10 individual blocks can be traded for one long base-10 rod. Then she asks the students to explain what she just modeled. One student replies, "We traded."

Analysis: Ms. Akbar provided guided intervention to scaffold student understanding. Students now have the opportunity to see that trading 10 individual blocks for 1 base-10 rod is a more efficient way to keep track and count. Also, students have the opportunity to make connections with standard notation for adding two-digit numbers. Furthermore, students can make connections between the written symbols and the model to understand regrouping.

Teacher Reflection

In video clip 6.2, Ms. Akbar reflects on the lesson and explains the prior knowledge that students had, their reasoning strategies, her mathematical goals, and what she would do differently next time. When asked about the role of manipulatives in student explanations, Ms. Akbar observes that the manipulatives help students explain their thinking. She points out that it was hard for other students to understand the explanations by simply looking at the numbers alone.

Ms. Akbar: Some of them already knew what to do without realizing what they were doing. It is interesting because last week they could not do that. They had five or six digits in there that they were adding up instead of carrying. I am not sure when they transferred over. It was really hard to get them to state why they did what they did, without the extra one in the 10s place. I have half the class that understands it but do not know why they understand it. Then I have the other half that does not understand it. . . . I thought for sure that they would understand about adding with base-10 blocks. I did not know that [they did not understand] until we started discussing.

Analysis: Ms. Akbar used formative assessment to make decisions on how to facilitate the discussion. She used several strategies such as listening to student explanations and having students demonstrate their understanding by explaining with models and writing. Also, she did quick surveys of class understanding by having students show if they agreed with something or disagreed by giving a thumbs up or thumbs down. Using these methods, she was able to identify that "half the students got it" but did not quite understand "why" the other half were confused. Besides, she also reflected on what she would do during her next discussion, concluding that she needs to spend more time with the students going over the place value and trading concepts. She explained that she could plan a lesson only two days in advance because the discussions drive what must be covered in the next day's lesson. Reflecting is valuable for thinking about what the students understand and don't understand and for mapping out your next steps.

Reflecting on Practice

Next Steps after a Whole Class Discussion

1. What errors and misconceptions did students have during the discussion? How can you check their understanding in the next lessons?

2. What mathematical insights did students gain during the lesson? Consider how you can build on these new insights.

3. What areas of student participation can be improved? How can you assess whether students understand the reasoning of their peers?

4. What are the goals of the next lesson? Do they build on the goals and skills in this lesson?

5. What additional considerations and concerns do you have?

STRATEGIES FOR THE CLASSROOM

Strategies to Refine and Improve Whole Class Discussion

- Videotape a lesson and analyze what is working and what needs improvement.
- Ask colleagues to observe a lesson and offer feedback.
- Observe another teacher's classroom to gain insights into other methods.
- Work with a math coach or lead teacher.
- Focus on one specific area at a time.
- Take small steps and work on them until you get results.

CHAPTER 7

Rubric for Self-Evaluation of Whole Class Discussion

Name: _____ Date: _____

Table 7.1   Self-Evaluation Rubric

	4 All the time	3 Sometimes	2 Sort of	1 Never
I clearly explain my thinking to others.				
I listen and think about other student explanations.				
I analyze and think critically about other explanations presented.				
I reflect on my strategy when listening to others.				

Comments about what I learned:

_____

_____

_____

_____

_____

_____

CHAPTER 7

Checklist for Classroom Observation

Name: _____ Observed by: _____
 Date:_____
 Check areas observed or focus of observation:

Table 7.2   Classroom Observation Checklist

Classroom Interactions   Comments
Nature of student participation _____
Teacher Questioning _____
Student Engagement _____

Student Understanding/Sense-Making
Focus on "big ideas," errors,
  misconceptions, or strategies to solve
  problems _____
The logical progression of conversation to
  develop more sophisticated mathematical
  ideas _____
Students critique, reflect, and ask questions
  on ideas presented _____

Teacher Interactions
Poses questions to facilitate thinking or
  clarification_____
Checks for student's understanding

_____
Adjusts conversation based on student's
  responses_____
Introduces new information based
  on student's current understanding

_____

Physical Classroom Environment
Organization of space for discussion

_____
Access to materials for discussion

_____
Space to display multiple solutions

_____

CHAPTER 7

Self-Reflection Checklist for Evaluating Whole Class Discussions

Table 7.3   Self-Reflection Checklist for Evaluating Whole Class Discussions

	Evidence/Observations	Notes:
Areas of strength		
Areas of growth		
Goals for improving discussion	Strategies to try	Notes:
1._____		
2._____		
3._____		

Comments: _____

_____

_____

References

Baroody, A. J., Feil, Y., & Johnson, A. R. (2011). An alternative reconceptualization of procedural and conceptual knowledge. *Journal for research in mathematics education*, 115–131.

Bertolone-Smith, C. M., & Gillette-Koyen, L. (2019). Making mathematical discourse worth your while. *Teaching Children Mathematics, 25*(4), 242–248.

Boaler, J. (1997). *Experiencing school mathematics: Teaching styles, sex and setting.* Buckingham, England: Open University Press.

Boaler, J., & Brodie, K. (2004). The importance, nature, and impact of teacher question. In D. E. McDougall & J. A. Ross (Eds.), Proceedings of the Twenty-Sixth Annual Meeting of the North American Chapter of the International Group for Psychology of Mathematics Education, Vol. 2 (pp. 773–782). Toronto, Ontario.

Boaler, J., & Greeno, J. (2000). Identity, agency and knowing in mathematical worlds. In J. Boaler (Ed.), *Multiple perspectives on mathematics teaching and learning.* Westport, CT: Ablex.

Bochicchio, D., Cole, B., Ostien, D., Rodriguez, V., Staples, M., Susiz, P., & Truxaw, M. (2009). Language. *Mathematics Teacher, 102*(8), 607–613.

Bray, W. (2011). A collective case study of the influences of teachers' beliefs and knowledge on error handling practices during class discussion of mathematics. *Journal for Research in Mathematics Education, 42*(1), 2–38.

Brown, S., & Walter, M. (2005). *The art of problem posing.* Mahwah, NJ: Lawrence Erlbaum Associates.

Bybee, R. (1997). *Achieving scientific literacy: From purposes to practices.* Portsmouth, NH: Heinemann.

Chapin, S., O'Connor, C., & Anderson, N. (2009). *Classroom discussions: Using math talk to help students learn.* Sausalito, CA: Math Solutions.

Cobb, P., Stephan, M., McClain, K., & Gravemeijer, K. (2001). Participating in classroom mathematical practices. *Journal of Learning Sciences, 10,* 113–164.

Cobb, P., Yackel, E., & McClain, K. (Eds.) (2000). *Communicating and symbolizing in mathematics: Perspectives on discourse, tools, and instructional design.* Mahwah, NJ: Lawrence Erlbaum Associates.

Council of Chief State School Officers, National Governors Association Center for Best Practices. (2010). *Common Core State Standards Mathematics.* Washington, DC: National Governors Association Center for Best Practices, Council of Chief State School Officers. Retrieved from http://www.corestandards.org/Math/Practice/

Fernandez, C. (2002). Learning from Japanese approaches to professional development: The case of lesson study. *Journal of Teacher Education, 53,* 393–405.

Gravemeijer, K., & van Galen, F. (2003). Facts and algorithms as products of students' own mathematical activity. In J. Kilpatrick, W. G. Martin, & D. Schifter (Eds.), *A research companion to principles and standards for school mathematics* (pp. 114–122). Reston, VA: National Council of Teachers of Mathematics (NCTM).

Hardin, C. (2011). *Effective classroom management: Models and strategies for today's classrooms.* Boston: Pearson.

Hiebert, J. (2003). Signposts for teaching mathematics through problem solving. In F. K. Lester, Jr. & R. Charles (Eds.), *Teaching mathematics through problem solving, grades prekindergarten–grade 6* (pp. 53–61). Reston, VA: NCTM.

Hiebert, J., Carpenter, T. P., Fennema, E., Fuson, K.C., Wearne, D., Murray, H., Human, P., & Olivier, A. (1997). *Making sense: Teaching and learning mathematics with understanding.* Portsmouth, NH: Heinemann.

Jacobs, V., Lamb, L., & Philipp, R. (2010). Professional noticing of children's mathematical thinking. *Journal for Research in Mathematics Education, 41*(2), 169–202.

Jenson, A. (2008). An investigation of relationships between seventh-grade students' belief and their participation during mathematics discussions in two classrooms. *Mathematical Thinking and Learning, 10,* 68–100.

Kilpatrick, J., Swafford, J., & Findell, B. (2001). *Adding It Up: Helping Children Learn Mathematics.* Washington, DC: National Academy Press.

Larrivee, B. (2008). *Authentic classroom management: Creating a learning community and building reflective practice.* Boston, MA: Pearson.

Leinhardt, G., & Steele, M. D. (2005). Seeing the complexity of standing to the side: Instructional dialogues. *Cognition and Instruction, 23*(1), 87–163.

Lewis, C., Perry, R., & Hurd, J. (2009). Improving mathematics instruction through lesson study: A theoretical model and North American case. *Journal of Mathematics Teacher Education, 12*(4). 285–304.

Martino, A., & Maher, C. (1999). Teacher questioning to promote justification and generalization in mathematics: What research practice has taught us. *Journal of Mathematical Behavior, 1*(1), 53–76.

Nathan, M., & Knuth, E. (2003). A study of whole classroom mathematical discourse and teacher change. *Cognition and Instruction, 21*(2), 175–207.

National Council of Teachers of Mathematics. (2000). *Principles and standards for school mathematics.* Reston, VA: NCTM.

National Governors Association Center for Best Practices, & Council of Chief State School Officers. (2010). Common Core State Standards Initiative. (2010). Common core state standards for mathematics. http://www. corestandards. org/assets/ CCSSI_Math% 20Standards. pdf.

National Research Council. (2000). *How people learn: Brain, mind, experience, and school*, expanded edition. Washington, DC: National Academies Press.

National Research Council, & Mathematics Learning Study Committee. (2001). Adding it up: Helping children learn mathematics. National Academies Press.

National Research Council. (2019). *How people learn II*. Washington, DC: National Academies Press.

Novak, J. D., & Cañas, A. J. (2006). The theory underlying concept maps and how to construct them. Florida Institute for Human and Machine Cognition, 1, 2006–2001.

O'Connor, C., Michaels, S., Chapin, S., & Harbaugh, A. G. (2017). The silent and the vocal: Participation and learning in whole-class discussion. *Learning and Instruction, 48,* 5–13.

Patrick, H., Turner, J. C., Meyer, D. K., & Midgley, C. (2003). How teachers establish psychological environments during the first days of school: Associations with avoidance in mathematics. *Teachers College Record, 105,* 1521–1558.

Race, K. E., Ho, E., & Bower, L. (2002). *Documenting in-classroom support and coaching activities of a professional development program directed toward school-wide change: An integral part of an organization's evaluation efforts.* Paper presented at the annual meeting of the American Educational Research Association, New Orleans, LA.

Schoenfeld, A. H. (1998). Towards a theory of teaching-in-context. *Issue in Education, 4,* 1–94.

Smith, M. S., Bill, V., & Hughes, E. K. (2008). Thinking through a lesson: Successfully implementing high-level tasks. *Mathematics Teaching in the Middle School, 14*(3), 132–138.

Smith, M. S., & Stein, M. (2011). *5 practices for orchestrating productive mathematical discussions.* Reston, VA; and Thousand Oaks, CA: NCTM and Corwin Press.

Spiegel, D. (2005). Classroom discussion: Strategies for engaging all students, building higher-level thinking skills, and strengthening reading and writing across the curriculum. New York: Scholastic Inc.

Star, J. R. (2005). Reconceptualizing procedural knowledge. *Journal for Research in Mathematics Education, 36*(5), 404–411.

Stein, M. K., Engle, R. A., Smith, M. S., & Hughes, E. K. (2008). Orchestrating productive mathematical discussions: Helping teachers learn to better incorporate student thinking. *Mathematical Thinking and Learning, 10*(4), 313–340.

Van Zoest, L. R., Stockero, S. L., Leatham, K. R., Peterson, B. E., Atanga, N. A., & Ochieng, M. A. (2017). Attributes of instances of student mathematical thinking that are worth building on in whole-class discussion. *Mathematical Thinking and Learning, 19*(1), 33–54.

Wearne, D, Fennema, E, Murray, H, Hiebert, J, Fuson, K & Carpenter, T, 1(997). Making Sense: Teaching and Learning Mathematics with Understanding. Portsmouth,NJ: Heinemann.

Whitin, P., & Whitin, D. (2002). Promoting communication in the mathematics classroom. *Teaching Children Mathematics, 9*(4), 204–211.

Wong, H. K., & Wong, R.T. (2009). *The first days of school: How to be an effective teacher.* Mountain View, CA: Harry K. Wong Publications, Inc.

116   *References*

Yackel, E. (2003). Listening to children. In *Teaching mathematics through problem solving: Prekindergarten–grade 6* (pp.107–121). Reston, VA: NCTM.

Yackel, E., & Cobb, P. (1996). Sociomathematical norms, argumentations and autonomy in mathematics education. *Journal for Research in Mathematics Education, 27,* 458–477.

About the Author

Teruni D. Lamberg is an associate professor of elementary education at the University of Nevada, Reno. She teaches graduate and undergraduate mathematics education courses. She is the director of the Nevada Mathematics Initiative and the principal investigator and director of the Lemelson Math and Science Master's Cohort Program. She has also served as the principal investigator of the Northeastern Nevada Mathematics Project. Lamberg has worked with hundreds of teachers across the country to improve math teaching. Her mission is to provide teachers with tools and resources to support student learning through whole class discussions.

Lamberg spent many years in classrooms researching how to support teachers to conduct effective discussions. She discovered the importance of attending to the *process of teaching* to facilitate productive discussions that result in student achievement. Lamberg taught at elementary school before receiving her doctorate from Arizona State University and completing her post-doctorate work at Vanderbilt University.